LEADERSHIP

LEADERSHIP
THE ESSENTIAL GUIDE

NICCOLÒ MACHIAVELLI
The Prince

RALPH WALDO EMERSON
Power

SUN TZU
The Art of War

ABRIDGED AND INTRODUCED BY
MITCH HOROWITZ

MEDIA

Published by Gildan Media LLC
aka G&D Media.
www.GandDmedia.com

The Prince was first printed in 1532
Power was first published in Ralph Waldo Emerson's collection
The Conduct of Life in 1860
The Art of War is estimated to have been written c. 500 BC
The English translation by Lionel Giles was published 1910
G&D Media Condensed Classics editions published 2019
Abridgement and Introduction copyright © 2019 by Mitch
Horowitz

FIRST EDITION: 2019

Cover design by David Rheinhardt of Pyrographx

Interior design by Meghan Day Healey of Story Horse, LLC.

ISBN: 978-1-7225-0211-9

Contents

Introduction

The Meaning of Leadership
By Mitch Horowitz

What is good leadership? My personal view is that a good leader should never ask those who report to him to do anything that he wouldn't be willing to do himself. Also, a good leader should be able to take over a task himself—no matter how apparently menial—and should know how to do it. A leader who cannot ship a package or clean a toilet, or is unwilling to, is not a leader.

This came to me at a stage in my career when I was stripped of all assistance and left to do things for myself that I normally handed off to another. It meant ordering paperclips, taking random phone calls, and performing clerical tasks. At first my pride was wounded, and I was unsure of how to proceed. I soon learned a lesson in leadership that has remained with me ever since: a true leader never places him or herself above any task. I was reminded of the words of Napoleon, as recorded by Ralph Waldo Emerson in his 1860 essay *Success*:

> *"There is nothing in war,"* said Napoleon, *"which I cannot do by my own hands. If there is nobody to make gunpowder, I can manufacture it. The gun-carriages I know how to construct. If it is necessary to make cannons at the forge, I can make them. The details of working them in battle, if it is necessary to teach, I shall teach them. In administration, it is I alone who have arranged the finances, as you know."*

This is the spirit that I hope you discover in the condensed works in this collection. Each of them—*The Prince* by Niccolò Machiavelli, *Power* by Emerson, and *The Art of War* by Sun Tzu—shines its own light on a universal theme, that of self-sufficiency. The leader who cannot handle every contingency on his or her own is not a true leader but a kept figurehead. Fear and favoritism can be used to retain power in the pettiest sense, but the grasp is illusory. In such cases, you are a title-holder but not a figure of authority, and time will make this plain.

The influence of a leader should outlast his or her title or office. Because, like all things in life, a title and its privileges will suddenly or eventually be taken away. Your works themselves, and your impact on people around you, will alone remain. And in that legacy appears the true measure of your leadership.

Like all of the authors in this volume, seek posterity in whatever you do. In the end, the only thing that belongs to us is hard-won reputation. And as Renaissance-era writer Machiavelli notes: "They who come to the Princedom . . . by virtuous paths, acquire with difficulty, but keep with ease."

THE
PRINCE

THE
PRINCE

by Niccolò Machiavelli

*History's Greatest Guide to
Attaining and Keeping Power—
Now In a Special Condensation*

Abridged and Introduced
by Mitch Horowitz

THE CONDENSED 📖 CLASSICS LIBRARY™

Contents

A Different Side of *The Prince*

By Mitch Horowitz

It does not come naturally to me to introduce and abridge Niccolò Machiavelli's 1532 classic *The Prince*. The Renaissance-era guide to gaining and holding power has been known for centuries as a blueprint to ruthlessness, deception, and even brutality. I have inveighed against current books, like *The 48 Laws of Power*, that endorse amoral or unethical methods of personal advancement.

"But that's the real world," argue the defenders of such books. Not my world. And not the one I encourage others to dwell in.

How, then, do I justify this condensed and reader-friendly new edition of *The Prince*, a book considered the urtext of guides to ruthless attainment? The fact is—as you will discover in this careful abridgement—the writer and diplomat Machiavelli imbued his work with a greater sense of purpose and ethics than is commonly understood. Although Machiavelli unquestionably endorses absolutist and, at times, bloody ways of dealing with adversaries, he repeatedly notes that these are efforts of a last or near-last resort, when peaceable means of governance prove either unpromising or unworkable. He justifies resorting to deception or faithlessness only as a defense against the depravity of men, who shift alliances like the winds. This logic by no means approaches the morality of Christ's principle to be "wise as serpents and harmless as doves," but it belies the general notion that Machiavelli was a one-dimensional schemer.

Moreover, the author also emphasizes rewarding merit; leaving the public to its own devices and personal pursuits as much as possible (which is the essential ingredient to developing culture and economy); trusting subjects enough to allow them to bear arms—and even to arm them yourself if confident in their loyalty (which the good leader should be); surrounding oneself with wise counselors (the true measure of an able ruler); avoiding and not exploiting civic divisions; and striving to ensure the public's general satisfaction.

One of the most striking parts of the book for me is when Machiavelli expounds on the best kind of intellect for an adviser or minister. In chapter XVII he writes:

> *There are three scales of intelligence, one which understands by itself, a second which understands what it is shown by others, and a third, which understands neither by itself nor by the showing of others, the first of which is most excellent, the second good, but the third worthless.*

This has always been my favorite passage of Machiavelli's. To add a further dimension to his observation, here is an alternate translation (and I challenge you to consider what place you have earned on its scale):

> *There exist three kinds of intellects: that belonging to the one who can do the thing itself, that belonging to the one who can judge the thing, and that belonging to the one who can neither do nor judge. The first is excellent, the second is good, and the third is worthless.*

Some contemporary critics suggest that *The Prince* is actually a satire of monarchy: that under the guise of a guide to ruthless conduct Machiavelli sends up the actions of absolute rulers and covertly calls for more republican forms of government. I think this assessment probably stretches matters. But it would be equally wrong, as noted, to conclude that Machiavelli was a narrow-eyed courtier bent on keeping others down. On balance, Machiavelli was a pragmatic tutor interested in promoting the unity, stability, and integrity of nation states, chiefly his own Italy, in a Europe that lacked cohesive civics and reliable international treaties. His harsher ideas were then considered acceptable quivers in the bow of statecraft; you will also see his efforts to leaven them with keen observations about the vicissitudes of human nature, fate, and virtue.

In actuality, I believe that businesspeople, leaders, and entrepreneurs who read *The Prince* today will discover subtleties that are missing from current power-at-any-cost guides. I advise experiencing *The Prince* through the filter of your own ethical standards and inner truths; sifting among its practical lessons; taking in its tough observations about human weaknesses; and using it as a guide to the realities —and foibles—of how we live.

Let me say a brief word about my method of abridgment. First, I have used the 1910 translation of Renaissance scholar N.H. Thomson, which originally appeared as part of the Harvard Classics line. My aim in condensing Thomson's translation is to provide the full range of Machiavelli's lessons and observations, but without most of his historical portraiture (which is well worth reading in the original, if you are engaged by what you encounter here). I have taken Machiavelli's most relatable and practical passages and ordered them into individual segments, each with a new and clarifying title. I have striven to eliminate repetition. I have occasionally substituted modern terms for antiquated ones. Finally, I have included a closing section of Machiavelli's most poignant aphorisms.

I have found among my possessions none that I prize and esteem more than a knowledge of the actions of great men, acquired in the course of long experience in modern affairs and a continual study of antiquity. This knowledge has been most carefully and patiently pondered over and sifted by me, and now reduced into this little book. I can offer no better gift than the means of mastering, in a very brief time, all that in the course of so many years, and at the cost of so many hardships and dangers, I have learned, and know.

—Niccolò Machiavelli

Chapter I

On Acquiring a New Kingdom

The Prince cannot avoid giving offense to new subjects, either in respect of the troops he quarters on them, or of some other of the numberless vexations attendant on a new acquisition. And in this way you may find that you have enemies in all those whom you have injured in seizing the Princedom, yet cannot keep the friendship of those who helped you to gain it; since you can neither reward them as they expect, nor yet, being under obligations to them, use violent remedies against them. For however strong you may be in respect of your army, it is essential that in entering a new Province you should have the good will of its inhabitants.

Hence it happened that Louis XII of France speedily gained possession of Milan, and as speedily lost it. For the very people who had opened the gates to the French King, when they found themselves deceived in their expectations and hopes of future benefits, could not put up with the insolence of their new ruler.

True it is that when a State rebels and is again got under, it will not afterwards be lost so easily. For the Prince, using the rebellion as a pretext, will not hesitate to secure himself by punishing the guilty, bringing the suspected to trial, and otherwise strengthening his position in the points where it was weak.

I say, then, that those States which upon their acquisition are joined onto the ancient dominions of the Prince who acquires them are either of the same religion and language as the people of these dominions, or they are not. When they are, there is great ease in retaining them, especially when they have not been accustomed to live in freedom. To hold them securely it is enough to have rooted out the line of the reigning Prince; because if in other respects the old condition of things be continued, and there be no discordance in their customs, men live peaceably with one another. Even if there be some slight difference in their languages, provided that customs are similar, they can easily get on together. He, therefore, who acquires such a State, if he mean to keep it, must see to two things: first, that the blood of the ancient line of Princes be destroyed; second, that no change be made in respect of laws or taxes; for in this way the newly acquired State speedily becomes incorporated.

But when States are acquired in a country differing in language, usages, and laws, difficulties multiply, and great good fortune, as well as actions, are needed to overcome them. One of the best and most efficacious methods for dealing with such a State is for the Prince who acquires it to go and dwell there in person, since this will tend to make his tenure more secure and lasting. For when you are on the spot, disorders are detected in their beginnings and remedies can be readily applied; but when you are at a distance, they are not heard of until they have gathered strength and the case is past cure. Moreover, the Province in which you take up your abode is not pillaged by your officers; the people are pleased to have a ready recourse to their Prince; and have all the more reason if they are well disposed, to love, if disaffected, to fear him. A foreign enemy desiring to attack that State would be cautious how he did so. In short, where the Prince resides in person, it will be extremely difficult to oust him.

Another excellent expedient is to send colonies into one or two places, so that these may become, as it were, the keys of the Province; for you must either do this, or else keep up a numerous force of men-at-arms and foot soldiers. A Prince need not spend much on colonies. He can send them out and support them at little or no charge to himself, and the only persons to whom he gives offence are those whom he deprives of their fields and houses to bestow them on the new inhabitants. Those who are thus injured form but a small part of the community, and remaining scattered and poor can never become dangerous. All others being left unmolested, are in consequence easily quieted, and at the same time are afraid to make a false move, lest they share the fate of those who have been deprived of their possessions. In few words, these colonies cost less than soldiers, are more faithful, and give less offense, while those who are offended, being, as I have said, poor and dispersed, cannot hurt. And let it here be noted that men are either to be kindly treated, or utterly crushed, since they can revenge lighter injuries, but not graver. Wherefore the injury we do to a man should be of a sort to leave no fear of reprisals.

CHAPTER II

Against Occupation

If instead of colonies you send troops, the cost is vastly greater, and the whole revenues of the country are spent in guarding it; so that the gain becomes a loss, and much deeper offense is given; since in shifting the quarters of your soldiers from place to place the whole country suffers hardship, which as all feel, all are made enemies; and enemies who remaining, although vanquished, in their own homes, have power to hurt. In every way, therefore, this mode of defense is as disadvantageous as that by colonizing is useful.

In dealing with the countries of which they took possession the Romans diligently followed the methods I have described. They planted colonies, conciliated weaker powers without adding to their strength, humbled the great, and never suffered a formidable stranger to acquire influence.

CHAPTER III

The Example of Alexander the Great

A lexander the Great having achieved the conquest of Asia in a few years and, dying before he had well entered on possession, it might have been expected, given the difficulty of preserving newly acquired States, that on his death the whole country would rise in revolt.

Nevertheless, his successors were able to keep their hold, and found in doing so no other difficulty than arose from their own ambition and mutual jealousies.

If anyone think this strange and ask the cause, I answer that all the Princedoms of which we have record have been governed in one of two ways: 1) either by a sole Prince, all others being his servants permitted by his grace and favor to assist in governing the kingdom as his ministers; or 2) by a Prince with his Barons who hold their rank, not by the favor of a superior Lord, but by antiquity of bloodline, and who have States and subjects of their own who recognize them as their rulers and entertain for them a natural affection.

States governed by a sole Prince and by his servants—as with Alexander—vest in him a more complete authority; because throughout the land none but he is recognized as sovereign, and if obedience be yielded to any others, it is yielded as to his ministers and officers for whom personally no special love is felt.*

---

* Machiavelli is saying that civic and military authority surpasses bloodline.—MH

Chapter IV

How to Control Formerly Independent Territories

When a newly acquired State has been accustomed to live under its own laws and in freedom, there are three methods whereby it may be held. The first is to destroy it; the second, to go and reside there in person; the third, to suffer it to live on under its own laws, subjecting it to a tribute and entrusting its government to a few of the inhabitants who will keep the rest your friends. Such a Government, since it is the creature of the new Prince, will see that it cannot stand without his protection and support, and must therefore do all it can to maintain him; and a city accustomed to live in freedom, if it is to be preserved at all, is more easily controlled through its own citizens than in any other way.

We have examples of all these methods in the histories of the Spartans and the Romans. The Spartans

held Athens and Thebes by creating oligarchies in these
cities, yet lost them in the end. The Romans, to retain
Capua, Carthage, and Numantia, destroyed them and
never lost them. On the other hand, when they thought
to hold Greece as the Spartans had held it, leaving it
its freedom and allowing it to be governed by its own
laws, they failed, and had to destroy many cities of that
Province before they could secure it. For, in truth, there
is no sure way of holding other than by destroying,
and whoever becomes master of a City accustomed to
live in freedom and does not destroy it, may reckon on
being destroyed by it. For if it should rebel, it can always
screen itself under the name of liberty and its ancient
laws, which no length of time, nor any benefits conferred will ever cause it to forget; and do what you will,
and take what care you may, unless the inhabitants be
scattered and dispersed, this name, and the old order of
things, will never cease to be remembered, but will at
once be turned against you whenever misfortune over-
takes you.

If, however, the newly acquired City or Province
has been accustomed to live under a Prince, and his line
is extinguished, it will be impossible for the citizens,
used, on the one hand, to obey, and deprived, on the
other, of their old ruler, to agree to choose a leader from
among themselves; and as they know not how to live

as freemen, and are therefore slow to take up arms, a stranger may readily gain them over and attach them to his cause. But in Republics there is a stronger vitality, a fiercer hatred, a keener thirst for revenge. The memory of their former freedom will not let them rest; so that the safest course is either to destroy them, or to go and live in them.

CHAPTER V

When a Prince Conquers by Merit

Since men for the most part follow in the footsteps and imitate the actions of others, and yet are unable to adhere exactly to those paths which others have taken, or attain to the virtues of those whom they would resemble, the wise man should always follow the roads that have been trodden by the great, and imitate those who have most excelled, so that if he cannot reach their perfection, he may at least acquire something of its savor. Acting in this like the skillful archer, who seeing that the object he would hit is distant, and knowing the range of his bow, takes aim much above the destined mark; not designing that his arrow should strike so high, but that flying high it may strike the point intended.

I say, then, that in entirely new Princedoms where the Prince himself is new, the difficulty of maintaining possession varies with the greater or less ability of him who acquires possession. And, because the mere fact of a private person rising to be a Prince presupposes either merit or good fortune, it will be seen that the presence of one or other of these two conditions lessens, to some extent, many difficulties. And yet, he who is less beholden to Fortune has often in the end the better success; and it may be for the advantage of a Prince that, from his having no other territories, he is obliged to reside in person in the State which he has acquired.

Looking first to those who have become Princes by their merit and not by their good fortune, I say that the most excellent among them are Moses, Cyrus, Romulus, Theseus, and the like. And though perhaps I ought not to name Moses, he being merely an instrument for carrying out the Divine commands, he is still to be admired for those qualities which made him worthy to converse with God. But if we consider Cyrus and the others who have acquired or founded kingdoms, they will all be seen to be admirable. And if their actions and the particular institutions of which they were the authors be studied, they will be found not to differ from those of Moses, instructed though he was by so great a teacher. Moreover, on examining their lives and actions, we shall see that they were debtors to Fortune for nothing beyond the opportunity which enabled them to shape things as they pleased, without which the force of their spirit would have been spent in vain; as on the other hand, opportunity would have offered itself in vain had the capacity for turning it to account been wanting. It was necessary, therefore, that Moses should find the children of Israel in bondage in Egypt, and oppressed by the Egyptians, in order that they might be disposed to follow him, and so escape from their servitude. It was fortunate for Romulus that he found no home in Alba, but was exposed at the time of his birth, to the end that he might become king and founder of the City of Rome. It was necessary that Cyrus should find the Persians discontented with the rule of the Medes, and the Medes enervated and effeminate from a prolonged peace. Nor could Theseus have displayed his great qualities had he not found the Athenians disunited and dispersed. But while it was their opportunities that made these men fortunate, it was their own merit that enabled them to recognize these opportunities and turn them to account, to the glory and prosperity of their country.

They who come to the Princedom, as these did, by virtuous paths, acquire with difficulty, but keep with ease. The difficulties which they have in acquiring arise

mainly from the new laws and institutions that they
are forced to introduce in founding and securing their
government. And let it be noted that there is no more
delicate matter to take in hand, nor more dangerous
to conduct, nor more doubtful in its success, than to
set up as a leader in the introduction of changes. For
he who innovates will have for his enemies all those
who are well off under the existing order of things, and
only lukewarm supporters in those who might be better
off under the new. This lukewarm temper arises partly
from the fear of adversaries who have the laws on their
side, and partly from the incredulity of mankind, who
will never admit the merit of anything new, until they
have seen it proved by the event. The result, however, is
that whenever the enemies of change make an attack,
they do so with all the zeal of partisans, while the others
defend themselves so feebly as to endanger both themselves and their cause.

It should be borne in mind that the temper of the
multitude is fickle, and that while it is easy to persuade
them of a thing, it is hard to fix them in that persuasion.
Wherefore, matters should be so ordered that when
men no longer believe of their own accord, they may be
compelled to believe by force. Moses, Cyrus, Theseus,
and Romulus could never have made their ordinances
be observed for any length of time had they been un-

armed, as was the case, in our own days, with the Friar Girolamo Savonarola, whose new institutions came to nothing so soon as the multitude began to waver in their faith; since he had not the means to keep those who had been believers steadfast in their belief, or to make unbelievers believe.

Such persons, therefore, have great difficulty in carrying out their designs; but all their difficulties are on the road, and may be overcome by courage. Having conquered these, and coming to be held in reverence, and having destroyed all who were jealous of their influence, they remain powerful, safe, honored, and prosperous.

When a Prince Conquers with Help of Others or by Luck

They who from private life become Princes by mere good fortune, do so with little trouble, but have much trouble to maintain themselves. They meet with no hindrance on their way, being carried as it were on wings to their destination, but all their difficulties overtake them when they alight. Of this class are those on whom States are conferred either in return for money, or through the favor of him who confers them.

Such Princes are wholly dependent on the favor and fortunes of those who have made them great; of supports none could be less stable or secure; and they lack both the knowledge and the power that would enable them to maintain their position. They lack the knowledge because, unless they have great parts and force of character, it is not to be expected that having always lived in a private station they should have learned how to command. They lack the power since they cannot look for support from attached and faithful troops. Moreover, States suddenly acquired, like all else that is produced and grows up rapidly, can never have such root or hold as that the first storm which strikes them shall not overthrow them; unless, indeed that they who suddenly become Princes have a capacity for learning quickly how to defend what Fortune has placed in their lap, and can lay those foundations after they rise which by others are laid before.

He who does not lay his foundations at first, may, if he be of great ability, succeed in laying them afterwards, though with inconvenience to the builder and risk to the building.

A certain type of man will judge it necessary, on entering a new Princedom, to rid himself of enemies, to conciliate friends, to prevail by force or fraud, to make himself feared yet not hated by his subjects, respected and obeyed by his soldiers, to crush those who can or ought to injure him, to introduce changes in the old order of things, to be at once severe and affable, magnanimous and liberal, to do away with a mutinous army and create a new one, to maintain relations with Kings and Princes on such a footing that they must see it for their interest to aid him, and dangerous to offend.

CHAPTER VII

When a Prince Conquers by Crime

A man may also rise from privacy to be a Prince in one of two ways, neither of which can be ascribed wholly either to merit or to fortune. The ways I speak of are, first, when the ascent to power is made by paths of wickedness and crime; and, second, when a private person becomes ruler of his country by the favor of his fellow-citizens.

Whoever examines the first man's actions and achievements will discover little or nothing in them which can be ascribed to Fortune, seeing that it was not through the favor of any but by the regular steps of the military service, gained at the cost of a thousand hardships and hazards, he reached the princedom, which he afterwards maintained by so many daring and dangerous enterprises. Still, to slaughter fellow-citizens, to betray friends, to be devoid of honor, pity, and religion, cannot be counted as merits, for these are means which may lead to power, but which confer no glory.

On seizing a state, the usurper should make haste to inflict what injuries he must, at a stroke, that he may not have to renew them daily, but be enabled by their discontinuance to reassure men's minds and afterwards win them over by benefits. Whosoever, either through timidity or from following bad counsels adopts a contrary course must keep the sword always drawn, and can put no trust in his subjects, who suffering from continued and constantly renewed severities, will never yield him their confidence. Injuries, therefore, should be inflicted all at once that their ill savor being less lasting may the less offend; whereas, benefits should be conferred little by little that so they may be more fully relished.

But, above all things, a Prince should so live with his subjects that no vicissitude of good or evil fortune shall oblige him to alter his behavior; because, if a need to change should come through adversity, it is then too late to resort to severity; while any leniency that you may use will be thrown away, for it will be seen to be compulsory and gain you no thanks.

CHAPTER VIII

When a Prince Rules
by Popular Consent

I come now to the second case, namely, of the leading citizen who, not by crimes or violence, but by the favor of his fellow-citizens is made Prince of his country. This may be called a Civil Princedom, and its attainment depends not wholly on merit, nor wholly on good fortune, but rather on what may be termed a fortunate astuteness. I say then that the road to this Princedom lies either through the favor of the people or of the nobles. For in every city are to be found these two opposed humors having their origin in this: that the people desire not to be domineered over or oppressed by the nobles, while the nobles desire to oppress and domineer over the people. And from these two contrary appetites there arises in cities one of three results: a Princedom, or Liberty, or License. A Princedom is cre-

ated either by the people or by the nobles, according as
one or other of these factions has occasion for it. For
when the nobles perceive that they cannot withstand
the people, they set to work to magnify the reputation
of one of their number, and make him their Prince, to
the end that under his shadow they may be enabled to
indulge their desires. The people, on the other hand,
when they see that they cannot make head against the
nobles, invest a single citizen with all their influence
and make him Prince, that they may have the shelter of
his authority.

He who is made Prince by the favor of the nobles,
has greater difficulty to maintain himself than he who
comes to the Princedom by aid of the people, since he
finds many about him who think themselves as good
as he, and whom, on that account, he cannot guide or
govern as he would. But he who reaches the Princedom
by the popular support, finds himself alone, with none,
or but a very few about him who are not ready to obey.
Moreover, the demands of the nobles cannot be satisfied
with credit to the Prince, nor without injury to others,
while those of the people well may, the aim of the people
being more honorable than that of the nobles, the latter
seeking to oppress, the former not to be oppressed. Add
to this, that a Prince can never secure himself against a
disaffected people, their number being too great, while

he may against a disaffected nobility, since their number is small. The worst that a Prince need fear from a disaffected people is that they may desert him, whereas when the nobles are his enemies he has to fear not only that they may desert him but also that they may turn against him; because, as they have greater craft and foresight, they always choose their time to suit their safety, and seek favor with the side they think will win. Again, a Prince must always live with the same people but need not always live with the same nobles, being able to make and unmake these from day to day, and give and take away their authority at his pleasure.

But to make this part of the matter clearer, I say that as regards the nobles there is this first distinction to be made. They either so govern their conduct as to bind themselves wholly to your fortunes, or they do not. Those who so bind themselves, and who are not grasping, should be loved and honored. As to those who do not so bind themselves, there is this further distinction. For the most part they are held back by pusillanimity and a natural defect of courage, in which case you should make use of them, and of those among them more especially who are prudent, for they will do you honor in prosperity, and in adversity give you no cause for fear. But where they abstain from attaching themselves to you of set purpose and for ambitious ends, it is a sign that they are thinking more of themselves than of you, and against such men a Prince should be on his guard, and treat them as though they were declared enemies, for in his adversity they will always help to ruin him.

He who becomes a Prince through the favor of the people should always keep on good terms with them; which it is easy for him to do, since all they ask is not to be oppressed. But he who against the will of the people is made a Prince by the favor of the nobles, must, above all things, seek to conciliate the people, which he readily may by taking them under his protection. For since men who are well treated by one whom they expected to treat them ill feel the more beholden to their benefactor, the people will at once become better disposed to such a Prince when he protects them than if he owed his Princedom to them.

There are many ways in which a Prince may gain the goodwill of the people, but, because these vary with circumstances, no certain rule can be laid down respecting them, and I shall, therefore, say no more about them. But this is the sum of the matter, that it is essential for a Prince to be on a friendly footing with his people since otherwise he will have no resource in adversity.

And what I affirm let no one controvert by citing the old saw that 'he who builds on the people builds on mire,' for that may be true of a private citizen who presumes on his favor with the people, and counts on being rescued by them when overpowered by his enemies or by the magistrates. In such cases a man may often find himself deceived. But when he who builds on the people is a Prince capable of command, of a spirit not to be cast down by ill-fortune, who, while he animates the whole community by his courage and bearing, neglects no prudent precaution, he will not find himself betrayed by the people, but will be seen to have laid his foundations well.

The most critical juncture for Princedoms of this kind, is at the moment when they are about to pass from the popular to the absolute form of government: and as these Princes exercise their authority either directly or through the agency of the magistrates, in the latter case their position is weaker and more hazardous, since they are wholly in the power of those citizens to whom the magistracies are entrusted, who can, and especially in difficult times with the greatest ease, deprive them of their authority, either by opposing or by not obeying them. And in times of peril it is too late for a Prince to assume to himself an absolute authority, for the citizens and subjects who are accustomed to take their orders from the magistrates will not when dangers threaten take them from the Prince, so that at such seasons there will always be very few in whom he can trust.

Such Princes, therefore, must not build on what they see in tranquil times when the citizens feel the need of the State. For then everyone is ready to run, to promise, and, danger of death being remote, even to die for the State. But in troubled times, when the State has need of its citizens, few of them are to be found. And the risk of the experiment is the greater in that it can only be made once. Wherefore, a wise Prince should devise means whereby his subjects may at all times, whether favorable or adverse, feel the need of the State and of him, and then they will always be faithful to him.

Chapter IX

How the Strength of Princedoms Should Be Measured

In examining the character of these Princedoms, another circumstance has to be considered, namely, whether the Prince is strong enough, if occasion demands, to stand alone, or whether he needs continual help from others. To make the matter clearer, I pronounce those to be able to stand alone who, with the men and money at their disposal, can get together an army fit to take the field against any assailant; and, conversely, I judge those to be in constant need of help who cannot take the field against their enemies, but are obliged to retire behind their walls, and to defend themselves there. As to the latter there is nothing to be said, except to exhort such Princes to strengthen and fortify the towns in which they dwell, and take no heed of the country outside. For whoever has thoroughly fortified his town, and put himself on such a footing with his subjects as I have already indicated and shall further speak of, will always be attacked with much caution; for men are always averse to enterprises that are attended with difficulty, and it is impossible not to foresee difficulties in attacking a Prince whose town is strongly fortified and who is not hated by his subjects.

A Prince, therefore, who has a strong city, and who does not make himself hated, cannot be attacked, or should he be so, his assailant will come badly off, since human affairs are so variable that it is almost impossible for anyone to keep an army posted for a whole year without interruption of some sort. Should it be objected that if the citizens have possessions outside the town and see them burned they will lose patience, and that self-interest, together with the hardships of a protracted siege, will cause them to forget their loyalty, I answer that a capable and courageous Prince will always overcome these difficulties by holding out hopes to his subjects that the evil will not be of long continuance; by exciting their fears of the enemy's cruelty; and by dexterously silencing those who seem to him too forward in their complaints. Moreover, it is to be expected that the enemy will burn and lay waste the country immediately on their arrival, at a time when men's minds are still heated and resolute for defense. And for this very reason the Prince has less to fear because after a few days, when the first ardor has abated, the injury is already done and suffered and cannot be undone; and the people will now, all the more readily, make common cause with their Prince from his seeming to be under obligations to them, their houses having been burned and their lands wasted in his defense. For it is the nature of men to incur obligation as much by the benefits they render as by those they receive.

If the whole matter be well considered, it ought not to be difficult for a prudent Prince, both at the outset and afterwards, to maintain the spirits of his subjects during a siege; provided always that provisions and other means of defense do not run short.

CHAPTER X

Of Soldiers and Mercenaries

The arms with which a Prince defends his State are either his own subjects, or they are mercenaries, or they are auxiliaries, or they are partly one and partly another. Mercenaries and auxiliaries are at once useless and dangerous, and he who holds his State by means of mercenary troops can never be solidly or securely seated. For such troops are disunited, ambitious, insubordinate, treacherous, insolent among friends, cowardly before foes, and without fear of God or faith with man. Whenever they are attacked defeat follows; so that in peace you are plundered by them, in war by your enemies. And this is because they have no tie or motive to keep them in the field beyond their paltry pay, in return for which it would be too much to expect them to give their lives. They are ready enough, therefore, to be your soldiers while you are at peace, but when war is declared they make off and disappear.

I ought to have little difficulty in getting this believed, for the present ruin of Italy is due to no other cause than her having for many years trusted to mercenaries, who though heretofore they may have helped the fortunes of some one man, and made a show of strength when matched with one another, have always revealed themselves in their true colors so soon as foreign enemies appeared.

The second sort of unprofitable arms are auxiliaries, by whom I mean troops brought to help and protect you by a potentate whom you summon to your aid; as when in recent times, Pope Julius II, observing the pitiful behavior of his mercenaries at the enterprise of Ferrara, betook himself to auxiliaries, and arranged with Ferdinand of Spain to be supplied with horse and foot soldiers.*

Auxiliaries may be excellent and useful soldiers for themselves, but are always hurtful to him who calls them in; for if they are defeated, he is undone; if victorious, he becomes their prisoner. Ancient histories abound with instances of this.

Let him, therefore, who would deprive himself of every chance of success, have recourse to auxiliaries,

---

* Julius was later forced to make territorial concessions to Ferdinand. —MH

these being far more dangerous than mercenary arms, bringing ruin with them ready made. For they are united, and wholly under the control of their own officers; whereas, before mercenaries, even after gaining a victory, can do you hurt, longer time and better opportunities are needed; because, as they are made up of separate companies, raised and paid by you, he whom you place in command cannot at once acquire such authority over them as will be injurious to you. In short, with mercenaries your greatest danger is from their inertness and cowardice, with auxiliaries from their valor. Wise Princes, therefore, have always eschewed these arms, and trusted rather to their own, and have preferred defeat with the latter to victory with the former, counting that as no true victory which is gained by foreign aid.

CHAPTER XI

The Prince and Military Affairs

A Prince, therefore, should have no care or thought other than for war, and for the regulations and training it requires, and should apply himself exclusively to this as his peculiar province; for war is the sole art looked for in one who rules, and is of such efficacy that it not merely maintains those who are born Princes, but often enables men to rise to that eminence from a private station; while, on the other hand, we often see that when Princes devote themselves rather to pleasure than to arms, they lose their dominions. And as neglect of this art is the prime cause of such calamities, to be proficient in it is the surest way to acquire power.

Between an armed and an unarmed man no proportion holds, and it is contrary to reason to expect that the armed man should voluntarily submit to him who is unarmed, or that the unarmed man should stand secure among armed retainers. For with contempt on one side and distrust on the other it is impossible that men should work well together. Wherefore, as has already been said, a Prince who is ignorant of military affairs, besides other disadvantages, can neither be respected by his soldiers, nor can he trust them. A Prince, therefore, ought never to allow his attention to be diverted from warlike pursuits, and should occupy himself with them even more in peace than in war. This he can do in two ways, by practice or by study.

As to the practice, he ought, besides keeping his soldiers well trained and disciplined, to be constantly engaged in the chase, that he may inure his body to hardships and fatigue, and gain at the same time a knowledge of places, by observing how the mountains slope, the valleys open, and the plains spread; acquainting himself with the characters of rivers and marshes, and giving the greatest attention to this subject. Such knowledge is useful to him in two ways; for first, he learns thereby to know his own country, and to understand better how it may be defended; and next, from his familiar acquaintance with its localities, he readily comprehends the character of other districts when obliged to observe them for the first time. For the hills, valleys, plains, rivers, and marshes of Tuscany, for example, have a certain resemblance to those elsewhere;

so that from a knowledge of the natural features of that province, similar knowledge in respect of other provinces may readily be gained. The Prince who is wanting in this kind of knowledge, is wanting in the first qualification of a good captain for by it he is taught how to surprise an enemy, how to choose an encampment, how to lead his army on a march, how to array it for battle, and how to post it to the best advantage for a siege.

Among the commendations that Philopoemen, Prince of the Achaeans, has received from historians is this: that in times of peace he was always thinking of methods of warfare, so that when walking in the country with his friends he would often stop and talk with them on the subject. "If the enemy," he would say, "were posted on that hill, and we found ourselves here with our army, which of us would have the better position? How could we most safely and in the best order advance to meet them? If we had to retreat, what direction should we take? If they retired, how should we pursue?" In this way he put to his friends, as he went along, all the contingencies that can befall an army. He listened to their opinions, stated his own, and supported them with reasons; and from his being constantly occupied with such meditations, it resulted, that when in actual command no complication could ever present itself with which he was not prepared to deal.

As to the mental training of which we have spoken, a Prince should read histories, and in these should note the actions of great men, observe how they conducted themselves in their wars, and examine the causes of their victories and defeats. And above all, he should, as many great men of past ages have done, assume for his models those persons who before his time have been renowned and celebrated, whose deeds and achievements he should constantly keep in mind.

A wise Prince, therefore, should pursue such methods as these, never resting idle in times of peace but strenuously seeking to turn them to account, so that he may derive strength from them in the hour of danger, and find himself ready should Fortune turn against him.

CHAPTER XII

Better to Be Loved or Feared?

I say that every Prince should desire to be accounted merciful and not cruel. Nevertheless, he should be on his guard against the abuse of this quality of mercy.

A Prince should disregard the reproach of being thought cruel where it enables him to keep his subjects united and obedient. For he who quells disorder by a very few signal examples will in the end be more merciful than he who from too great leniency permits things to take their course and so to result in pillage and bloodshed; for these hurt the whole State, whereas the severities of the Prince injure individuals only. And for a new Prince, of all others, it is impossible to escape a name for cruelty, since new States are full of dangers.

Nevertheless, the new Prince should not be too ready of belief, nor too easily set in motion; nor should he himself be the first to raise alarms; but should so temper prudence with kindliness that too great confidence in others shall not throw him off his guard nor groundless distrust render him insupportable.

And here comes in the question whether it is better to be loved rather than feared, or feared rather than loved. It might perhaps be answered that we should wish to be both; but since love and fear can hardly exist together, if we must choose between them, it is far safer to be feared than loved. For of men it may generally be affirmed that they are thankless, fickle, false, studious to avoid danger, greedy of gain, devoted to you while you are able to confer benefits upon them, and ready, as I said before, while danger is distant, to shed their blood, and sacrifice their property, their lives, and their children for you; but in the hour of need they turn against you. The Prince, therefore, who without otherwise securing himself builds wholly on their professions is undone. For the friendships which we buy with a price, and do not gain by greatness and nobility of character, though they be fairly earned are not made good, but fail us when we have occasion to use them.

Moreover, men are less careful how they offend him who makes himself loved than him who makes himself feared. For love is held by the tie of obligation, which, because men are a sorry breed, is broken on every whisper of private interest; but fear is bound by the apprehension of punishment which never relaxes its grasp.

Nevertheless a Prince should inspire fear in such a fashion that if he do not win love he may escape hate. For a man may very well be feared and yet not hated, and this will be the case so long as he does not meddle with the property or with the women of his citizens and subjects. And if constrained to put any to death, he should do so only when there is manifest cause or reasonable justification. But, above all, he must abstain from seizing the property of others. For men will sooner forget the death of their father than the loss of their estate. Moreover, pretexts for confiscation are difficult to find, and he who has once begun to live by pillaging always finds reasons for taking what is not his; whereas reasons for shedding blood are fewer and sooner exhausted.

Among other things remarkable in Hannibal, this has been noted: that having a very great army, made up of men of many different nations and brought to fight in a foreign country, no dissension ever arose among the soldiers themselves, nor any mutiny against their leader, either in his good or in his evil fortunes. This we can only ascribe to the transcendent cruelty, which, joined with numberless great qualities, rendered him at once venerable and terrible in the eyes of his soldiers, for without this reputation for cruelty these other virtues would not have produced the like results.

CHAPTER XIII

Truth and Deception

Everyone understands how praiseworthy it is in a Prince to maintain trust, and to live uprightly and not craftily. Nevertheless, we see from what has taken place in our own days that Princes who have set little store by their word, but have known how to overreach men by their cunning, have accomplished great things, and in the end got the better of those who trusted to honest dealing.

Be it known, then, that there are two ways of contending, one in accordance with the laws, the other by force; the first of which is proper to men, the second to beasts. But since the first method is often ineffectual, it becomes necessary to resort to the second. A Prince should, therefore, understand how to use well both the man and the beast. And this lesson has been covertly taught by the ancient writers who relate how Achilles and many others of these old Princes were given over to be brought up and trained by Chiron the Centaur; the only meaning of their having for an instructor one who was half man and half beast is that it is necessary for a Prince to know how to use both natures, and that the one without the other has no stability.

But since a Prince should know how to use the beast's nature wisely, he ought of beasts to choose both the lion and the fox; for the lion cannot guard himself from the traps nor the fox from wolves. He must therefore be a fox to discern traps and a lion to drive off wolves.

To rely wholly on the lion is unwise; and for this reason a prudent Prince neither can nor ought to keep his word when to keep it is hurtful to him, and the causes which led him to pledge it are removed. If all men were good this would not be good advice, but since they are dishonest and do not keep faith with you, you in return need not keep faith with them; and no prince was ever at a loss for plausible reasons to cloak a breach of faith. Of this numberless recent instances could be given, and it might be shown how many solemn treaties and engagements have been rendered inoperative and idle through want of faith in Princes, and that he who was best known to play the fox has had the best success.

It is necessary, indeed, to put a good color on this nature, and to be skillful in simulating and dissembling.

But men are so simple, and governed so absolutely by their present needs, that he who wishes to deceive will never fail in finding willing dupes.

And you are to understand that a Prince, and most of all a new Prince, cannot observe all those rules of conduct in respect whereof men are accounted good, being often forced, in order to preserve his Princedom, to act in opposition to good faith, charity, humanity, and religion. He must therefore keep his mind ready to shift as the winds and tides of Fortune turn, and, as I have already said, he ought not to quit good courses if he can help it, but should know how to follow evil courses if he must.

A Prince should therefore be very careful that nothing ever escapes his lips that does not make him seem the embodiment of mercy, good faith, integrity, humanity, and religion. And there is no virtue which it is more necessary for him to seem to possess than this last; because men in general judge rather by the eye than by the hand, for everyone can see but few can touch. Everyone sees what you seem, but few know what you are, and these few dare not oppose themselves to the opinion of the many who have the majesty of the State to back them up.

Moreover, in the actions of all men, and most of all of Princes, where there is no tribunal to which we can

appeal we look to results. Wherefore if a Prince succeeds in establishing and maintaining his authority the
means will always be judged honorable and be approved
by everyone. For the vulgar are always taken by appearances and by results, and the world is made up of the
vulgar, the few only finding room when the many have
no longer ground to stand on.

A certain Prince of our own days, whose name it
is as well not to mention, is always preaching peace
and good faith, although the mortal enemy of both;
and both, had he practiced them as he preaches them,
would, oftener than once, have lost him his kingdom
and authority.

CHAPTER XIV

How to Avert Conspiracies

Prince should consider how he may avoid such courses as would make him hated or despised; and that whenever he succeeds in keeping clear of these, he has performed his part, and runs no risk though he incur other infamies.

A Prince, as I have said before, sooner becomes hated by being rapacious and by interfering with the property and with the women of his subjects than in any other way. From these, therefore, he should abstain. For so long as neither their property nor their honor are touched the mass of mankind live contentedly, and the Prince has only to cope with the ambition of a few, which can in many ways and easily be kept within bounds.

A Prince is despised when he is seen to be fickle, frivolous, effeminate, pusillanimous, or irresolute, against which defects he ought therefore most carefully to guard, striving so to bear himself that greatness, courage, wisdom, and strength may appear in all his actions. In his private dealings with his subjects his decisions should be irrevocable, and his reputation such that no one would dream of overreaching or cajoling him.

The Prince who inspires such an opinion of himself is greatly esteemed, and against one who is greatly esteemed conspiracy is difficult; nor, when he is known to be an excellent Prince and held in reverence by his subjects, will it be easy to attack him. For a Prince is exposed to two dangers: from within in respect of his subjects, and from without in respect of foreign powers. Against the latter he will defend himself with good arms and good allies, and if he have good arms he will always have good allies; and when things are settled abroad, they will always be settled at home, unless disturbed by conspiracies; and even should there be hostility from without, if he has taken those measures, and has lived in the way I have recommended, and if he never abandons hope, he will withstand every attack.

As regards his own subjects, when affairs are quiet abroad, he has to fear they may engage in secret plots; against which a Prince best secures himself when he escapes being hated or despised, and keeps on good terms with his people; and this, as I have already shown, is essential. Not to be hated or despised by the body of his subjects is one of the surest safeguards that a Prince can have against conspiracy. For he who conspires always reckons on pleasing the people by putting the Prince to death; but when he sees that instead of pleasing he will offend them, he cannot summon courage to carry out his design. For the difficulties that attend conspirators are infinite, and we know from experience that while there have been many conspiracies, few of them have succeeded.

He who conspires cannot do so alone, nor can he assume as his companions any save those whom he believes to be discontented; but so soon as you impart your design to a discontented man, you supply him with the means of removing his discontent, since by betraying you he can procure for himself every advantage; so that seeing on the one hand certain gain and on the other a doubtful and dangerous risk, he must either be a rare friend to you or the mortal enemy of his Prince, if he keep your secret.

To put the matter shortly, I say that on the side of the conspirator there are distrust, jealousy, and dread of punishment to deter him; while on the side of the Prince there are the laws, the majesty of the throne, the protection of friends and of the government to defend him, to which if the general goodwill of the people be added, it is hardly possible that any should be rash enough to conspire. For while in ordinary cases,

the conspirator has ground for fear only before the ex-
ecution of his villainy, in this case he has also cause to
fear after the crime has been perpetrated since he has
the people for his enemy and is thus cut off from every
hope of shelter.

In brief, a Prince has little to fear from conspiracies when his subjects are well disposed towards him;
but when they are hostile and hold him in detestation
he has then reason to fear everything and everyone.
And well ordered States and wise Princes have provided with extreme care that the nobility shall not be
driven to desperation, and that the commons shall
be kept satisfied and contented; for this is one of the
most important matters that a Prince must look to.

CHAPTER XV

How a Prince
Should Defend Himself

To govern more securely some Princes have disarmed their subjects, others have kept the towns subject to them divided by factions; some have fostered hostility against themselves, others have sought to gain over those who at the beginning of their reign were looked on with suspicion; some have built fortresses, others have dismantled and destroyed them; and though no definite judgment can be pronounced respecting any of these methods, without regard to the special circumstances of the State to which it is proposed to apply them, I shall nevertheless speak of them in as comprehensive a way as the subject will admit.

It has never chanced that any new Prince has disarmed his subjects. On the contrary, when he has found them unarmed he has always armed them. For the arms thus provided become yours, those whom you suspected grow faithful, while those who were faithful at the first continue so, and from your subjects become your partisans. And though all your subjects cannot be armed yet if those of them whom you arm be treated with marked favor you can deal more securely with the rest. For the difference which those whom you supply with arms perceive in their treatment will bind them to you, while the others will excuse you recognizing that those who incur greater risk and responsibility merit greater rewards. But by disarming, you at once give offense, since you show your subjects that you distrust them, either as doubting their courage or as doubting their fidelity, each of which imputations begets hatred against you. Moreover, as you cannot maintain yourself without arms you must have recourse to mercenary troops. What these are I have already shown, but even if they were good, they could never avail to defend you at once against powerful enemies abroad and against subjects whom you distrust. Wherefore, as I have said already, new Princes in new Princedoms have always provided for their being armed; and of instances of this History is full.

But when a Prince acquires a new State, which thus becomes joined on like a limb to his old possessions, he must disarm its inhabitants, except such of them as have taken part with him while he was acquiring it; and even these, as time and occasion serve, he should seek to render soft and effeminate; and he must so manage matters that all the arms of the new State shall be in the hands of his own soldiers who have served under him in his ancient dominions.

I do not believe that divisions purposely caused can ever lead to good; on the contrary, when an enemy approaches, divided cities are lost at once, for the weaker faction will always side with the invader, and the other will not be able to stand alone.

Moreover methods like these argue weakness in a Prince, for under a strong government divisions would never be permitted, since they are profitable only in time of peace as an expedient whereby subjects may be more easily managed; but when war breaks out their insufficiency is demonstrated.

It has been customary for Princes, with a view to hold their dominions more securely, to build fortresses which might serve as a curb and restraint on such as have designs against them, and as a safe refuge against a first onset. I approve this custom, because it has been followed from the earliest times.

Fortresses are useful or not according to circumstances, and if in one way they benefit, in another they injure you. We may state the case thus: the Prince who is more afraid of his subjects than of strangers ought to build fortresses, while he who is more afraid of strangers than of his subjects should leave them alone.

All considerations taken into account, I shall applaud him who builds fortresses and him who does not; but I shall blame him who, trusting in them, reckons it a light thing to be held in hatred by his people.

CHAPTER XVI

How a Prince Should Preserve His Reputation

Nothing makes a Prince so well thought of as to undertake great enterprises and give striking proofs of his capacity.

It greatly profits a Prince in conducting the internal government of his State to follow striking methods. The remarkable actions of anyone in civil life, whether for good or for evil, afford him notability; and to choose such ways of rewarding and punishing cannot fail to be much spoken of. But above all, he should strive by all his actions to inspire a sense of his greatness and goodness.

A Prince is likewise esteemed who is a stanch friend and a thorough foe, that is to say, who without reserve openly declares for one against another, this being always a more advantageous course than to stand neutral.

For supposing two of your powerful neighbors come to blows, it must either be that you have, or have not, reason to fear the one who comes off victorious. In either case it will always be well for you to declare yourself, and join in frankly with one side or other. For should you fail to do so you are certain, in the former of the cases put, to become the prey of the victor to the satisfaction and delight of the vanquished, and no reason or circumstance that you may plead will avail to shield or shelter you; for the victor dislikes doubtful friends, and such as will not help him at a pinch; and the vanquished will have nothing to say to you, since you would not share his fortunes sword in hand.

A Prince should be careful never to join with one stronger than himself in attacking others, unless he is driven to it by necessity. For if he whom you join prevails, you are at his mercy; and Princes, so far as in them lies, should avoid placing themselves at the mercy of others.

A Prince should show himself a patron of merit, and should honor those who excel in every art. He ought accordingly to encourage his subjects by enabling them to pursue their callings, whether mercantile, agricultural, or any other, in security, so that this man shall not be deterred from beautifying his possessions from the apprehension that they may be taken from him, or that other refrain from opening a trade through fear of taxes; and he should provide rewards for those who desire so to employ themselves, and for all who are disposed in any way to add to the greatness of his City or State.

He ought, moreover, at suitable seasons of the year to entertain the people with festivals and shows. And because all cities are divided into guilds and companies, he should show attention to these societies, and sometimes take part in their meetings, offering an example of courtesy and munificence, but always maintaining the dignity of his station, which must under no circumstances be compromised.

CHAPTER XVII

A Prince's Court

The choice of Ministers is a matter of no small moment to a Prince. Whether they shall be good or not depends on his prudence, so that the readiest conjecture we can form of the character and sagacity of a Prince is from seeing what sort of men he has about him. When they are at once capable and faithful, we may always account him wise, since he has known to recognize their merit and to retain their fidelity. But if they be otherwise, we must pronounce unfavorably of him, since he has committed a first fault in making this selection.

There are three scales of intelligence, one which understands by itself, a second which understands what it is shown by others, and a third which understands neither by itself nor by the showing of others, the first of which is most excellent, the second good, but the third worthless.

As to how a Prince is to know his Minister, this unerring rule may be laid down. When you see a Minister
thinking more of himself than of you, and in all his
actions seeking his own ends, that man can never be a
good Minister or one that you can trust. For he who has
the charge of the State committed to him, ought not
to think of himself, but only of his Prince, and should
never bring to the notice of the latter what does not
directly concern him. On the other hand, to keep his
Minister good, the Prince should be considerate of him,
dignifying him, enriching him, binding him to himself
by benefits, and sharing with him the honors as well as
the burdens of the State, so that the abundant honors
and wealth bestowed upon him may divert him from
seeking them at other hands; while the great responsi-
bilities wherewith he is charged may lead him to dread
change, knowing that he cannot stand alone without
his master's support. When Prince and Minister are
upon this footing they can mutually trust one another;
but when the contrary is the case, it will always fare ill
with one or other of them.

CHAPTER XVIII

Flatterers Should Be Shunned

One error into which Princes, unless very prudent or very fortunate in their choice of friends, are apt to fall, is of so great importance that I must not pass it over. I mean in respect of flatterers. These abound in Courts, because men take such pleasure in their own concerns, and so deceive themselves with regard to them, that they can hardly escape this plague; while even in the effort to escape it there is risk of their incurring contempt.

For there is no way to guard against flattery but by letting it be seen that you take no offense in hearing the truth: but when everyone is free to tell you the truth respect falls short. Wherefore a prudent Prince should follow a middle course, by choosing certain discreet men from among his subjects, and allowing them alone free leave to speak their minds on any matter on which he asks their opinion, and on none other. But he ought to ask their opinion on everything, and after hearing what they have to say, should reflect and judge for himself. And with these counselors collectively, and with each of them separately, his bearing should be such, that each and all of them may know that the more freely they declare their thoughts the better they will be liked. Besides these, the Prince should hearken to no others, but should follow the course determined on, and afterwards adhere firmly to his resolves. Whoever acts otherwise is either undone by flatterers, or from continually vacillating as opinions vary, comes to be held in light esteem.

A Prince ought always to take counsel, but at such times and reasons only as he himself pleases, and not when it pleases others; nay, he should discourage every one from obtruding advice on matters on which it is not sought. But he should be free in asking advice, and afterwards as regards the matters on which he has asked it, a patient hearer of the truth, and even displeased should he perceive that any one, from whatever motive, keeps it back.

But those who think that every Prince who has a name for prudence owes it to the wise counselors he has around him, and not to any merit of his own, are certainly mistaken; since it is an unerring rule and of universal application that a Prince who is not wise himself cannot be well advised by others, unless by chance he surrender himself to be wholly governed by some one adviser who happens to be supremely prudent; in which case he may, indeed, be well advised; but not for long, since such an adviser will soon deprive him of his Government. If he listen to a multitude of advisers, the Prince who is not wise will never have consistent counsels, nor will he know of himself how to reconcile them. Each of his counselors will study his own advantage, and the Prince will be unable to detect or correct them. Nor could it well be otherwise, for men will always grow rogues on your hands unless they find themselves under a necessity to be honest.

Hence it follows that good counsels, whenever they come, have their origin in the prudence of the Prince, and not the prudence of the Prince in wise counsels.

CHAPTER XIX

The Role of Fortune

I am not ignorant that many have been and are of the opinion that human affairs are so governed by Fortune and by God that men cannot alter them by any prudence of theirs, and indeed have no remedy against them, and for this reason have come to think that it is not worthwhile to labour much about anything, but that they must leave everything to be determined by chance.

Often when I turn the matter over, I am in part inclined to agree with this opinion, which has had readier acceptance in our own times from the great changes in things which we have seen and everyday see happen contrary to all human expectation. Nevertheless, that our freewill be not wholly set aside, I think it may be the case that Fortune is the mistress of one half our actions, and yet leaves the control of the other half, or a little less, to ourselves. And I would liken her to one of those wild torrents which, when angry, overflow the plains, sweep away trees and houses, and carry off soil from one bank to throw it down upon the other. Everyone flees before them, and yields to their fury without the least power to resist. And yet, though this be their nature, it does not follow that in seasons of fair weather men cannot, by constructing dams and barriers, take such precautions as will cause them when again in flood to pass off by some artificial channel, or at least prevent their course from being so uncontrolled and destructive. And so it is with Fortune, who displays her might where there is no organized strength to resist her, and directs her onset where she knows that there is neither barrier nor embankment to confine her.

I note that one day we see a Prince prospering and the next day overthrown, without detecting any change in his nature or character. This, I believe, comes chiefly from a cause already dwelt upon, namely, that a Prince who rests wholly on Fortune is ruined when she changes. Moreover, I believe that he will prosper most whose mode of acting best adapts itself to the character of the times; and conversely that he will be unprosperous with whose mode of acting the times do not accord. For we see that men in these matters which lead to the end that each has before him, namely, glory and wealth, proceed by different ways, one with caution, another with impetuosity, one with violence, another with subtlety, one with patience, another with its contrary; and that by one or other of these different courses each may succeed.

Again, of two who act cautiously, you shall find that one attains his end, the other not, and that two of different temperament, the one cautious, the other impetuous, are equally successful. All which happens from no other cause than that the character of the times accords or does not accord with their methods of acting. And hence it comes, as I have already said, that two operating differently arrive at the same result, and two operating similarly, the one succeeds and the other not. On this likewise depend the vicissitudes of Fortune. For if to one who conducts himself with caution and patience, time and circumstances are propitious, so that his method of acting is good, he goes on prospering; but if these change he is ruined, because he does not change his method of acting.

For no man is found so prudent as to know how to adapt himself to these changes, both because he cannot deviate from the course to which nature inclines him, and because, having always prospered while adhering to one path, he cannot be persuaded that it would be well for him to forsake it. And so when occasion requires the cautious man to act impetuously, he cannot do so and is undone: whereas, had he changed his nature with time and circumstances, his fortune would have been unchanged.

To be brief, I say that since Fortune changes and men stand fixed in their old ways, they are prosperous so long as there is congruity between them, and the reverse when there is not. Of this, however, I am well persuaded, that it is better to be impetuous than cautious. For Fortune to be kept under must be beaten and roughly handled; and we see that she suffers herself to be more readily mastered by those who so treat her than by those who are more timid in their approaches. And always she favors the young, because they are less scrupulous and fiercer, and command her with greater audacity.

Chapter XX

Aphorisms from *The Prince*

"One change always leaves a dovetail into which another will fit."

"Men are either to be kindly treated or utterly crushed since they can revenge lighter injuries but not graver.

"The wise man should always follow the roads that have been trodden by the great, and imitate those who have most excelled."

"Take aim much above the destined mark."

"He who is less beholden to Fortune has often in the end the better success."

"Those who come to the Princedom by virtuous paths acquire with difficulty but keep with ease."

"It should be borne in mind that the temper of the multitude is fickle, and that while it is easy to persuade them of a thing, it is hard to fix them in that persuasion."

"He who does not lay his foundations at first, may, if he be of great ability, succeed in laying them afterwards, though with inconvenience to the builder and risk to the building."

"A Prince can never secure himself against a disaffected people, their number being too great, while he may against a disaffected nobility, since their number is small."

"Men are always averse to enterprises that are attended with difficulty."

"Mercenaries and auxiliaries are at once useless and dangerous, and he who holds his State by means of mercenary troops can never be solidly or securely seated."

"A Prince ought never to allow his attention to be diverted from warlike pursuits, and should occupy himself with them even more in peace than in war."

"Many Republics and Princedoms have been imagined that were never seen or known to exist in reality."

"If we must choose between them, it is far safer to be feared than loved."

"If a man have good arms he will always have good allies."

"I do not believe that divisions purposely caused can ever lead to good."

"A Prince should show himself a patron of merit."

"The readiest conjecture we can form of the character and sagacity of a Prince is from seeing what sort of men he has about him."

"A Prince who is not wise himself cannot be well advised by others."

"A Prince who rests wholly on Fortune is ruined when she changes."

"It is better to be impetuous than cautious. Fortune suffers herself to be more readily mastered by those who so treat her than by those who are timid in their approaches."

ABOUT THE AUTHORS

Born in Florence in 1469, NICCOLÒ MACHIAVELLI was
a widely travelled and deeply read diplomatic envoy for
Italy's royal court. Also a politician, historian, philosopher, humanist, writer, playwright, and poet, he has
been called the founder of modern political science for
his efforts to arrive at a cause-and-effect formula for
how to attain and hold power and conduct statecraft.
Machiavelli's classic *The Prince* was posthumously published in 1532. It was made up of earlier papers and letters that he had prepared for his royal patrons. A short
work of considerable innovation, *The Prince* is one of
the most enduring and widely read pieces of Renaissance literature. Although the term "Machiavellian"
came to refer to actions or people characterized by cunning ruthlessness, contemporary critics and scholars are
taking fuller note of Machiavelli's ethics and reformist
sympathies. The writer died in Florence at age 58 in
1527.

MITCH HOROWITZ is the PEN Award-winning author
of books including *Occult America* and *The Miracle
Club*. A writer-in-residence at the New York Public Li-

brary and lecturer-in-residence at the University of Philosophical Research in Los Angeles, Mitch introduces
and edits G&D Media's line of Condensed Classics
and is the author of the Napoleon Hill Success Course
series, including *The Miracle of a Definite Chief Aim*
and *The Power of the Master Mind*. Visit him at Mitch-
Horowitz.com.

POWER

POWER

by Ralph Waldo Emerson

The Immortal Classic on Will—
Now in Special Condensation

Abridged and Introduced
by Mitch Horowitz

THE CONDENSED CLASSICS LIBRARY™

Contents

Genius and Practicality

By Mitch Horowitz

Part of Ralph Waldo Emerson's greatness as a writer is that he never shied away from practicality. This was true of William James, as well. It can be argued that Emerson's most practical works—which include this essay on *Power*—were not among his greatest. Critic Irving Howe wrote that in such essays the philosopher "merely tugs the complexities . . . into the shallows of the explicit."

There is truth in this charge. And yet this judgment fails to take account of Emerson's bravery. Emerson felt obliged to be direct—to provide his readers with a plan of action. If this approach reduced philosophical complexities, it also banished authorial cowardice. Emerson would not dodge the question of how to practice the kinds of inner-reliance and self-driven living that his philosophical essays endorsed.

Hence, it is in *Power*, which Emerson published in his collection *The Conduct of Life* in 1860, that the Transcendentalist prescribed how and under what conditions a person can successfully assert his will in life.

Emerson identifies four essential elements to exercising personal power. The first—and that which sustains all the others—is to be "in sympathy with the course of things." Displaying his innate instinct for Taoism and other Eastern philosophies, Emerson believed that an individual could read the *nature of things* and seek to merge with it, like a twig carried downstream. "The mind that is parallel with the laws of nature," he writes, "will be in the current of events, and strong with their strength."

The second element of power is *health*. Emerson means this on different levels. He is speaking broadly of the vitality of body and spirit; the state of physicality and personal morale that sustains risks, seeks adventure, and completes plans. But he also speaks of routine bodily health, without which the individual's energies are sapped.

The third element is *concentration*. One of nature's laws is that concentration of energies brings impact. The concentration of a striking blow delivers the greatest force. Too often we deplete our energies by dispersing or spreading thin our aims and efforts. In *Power*, an imaginary oracle says: "Enlarge not thy destiny, endeavor not to do more than is given thee in charge." Like light focused in a laser, concentration into a single beam brings the greatest power.

The fourth and final element of power is *drilling*. By this Emerson means repeating a practice over and over until you can perform it with excellence. The martial artist repeats his movements and routines to the point where they enter his physical memory and are available to him under all conditions. Likewise, we must drill— or practice or rehearse—to the point where we have mastered our chosen task.

By entering the mechanics of practicality, did the philosopher lose some of his transcendental splendor? Some thought so; I see it differently. If Emerson had avoided such an approach he would have been guilty of failing to take his philosophy onto the road. Complexity is no excuse for inaction. And here I am reminded of an observation by the flawed and brilliant poet Ezra Pound, to whom I cede the last word: "But to have done instead of not doing/ This is not vanity."

I. Power

Who shall set a limit to the influence of a human being? There are men, who, by their sympathetic attractions, carry nations with them, and lead the activity of the human race. And if there be such a tie, that, wherever the mind of man goes, nature will accompany him, perhaps there are men whose magnetisms are of that force to draw material and elemental powers, and, where they appear, immense instrumentalities organize around them. Life is a search after power; and this is an element with which the world is so saturated,—there is no chink or crevice in which it is not lodged,—that no honest seeking goes unrewarded. A man should prize events and possessions as the ore in which this fine mineral is found; and he can well afford to let events and possessions, and the breath of the body go, if their value has been added to him in the shape of power. If he have secured the elixir, he can spare the wide gardens from which it was distilled. A cultivated man, wise to know and bold to perform, is the end to which nature works, and the education of the will is the flowering and result of all this geology and astronomy.

All successful men have agreed in one thing,— they were *causationists*. They believed that things went not by luck, but by law; that there was not a weak or a cracked link in the chain that joins the first and last of things. A belief in causality, or strict connection between every trifle and the principle of being, and, in consequence, belief in compensation, or, that nothing is got for nothing,—characterizes all valuable minds, and must control every effort that is made by an industrious one. The most valiant men are the best believers in the tension of the laws. "All the great captains," said Bonaparte, "have performed vast achievements by conforming with the rules of the art,—by adjusting efforts to obstacles."

The key to the age may be this, or that, or the other, as the young orators describe; —the key to all ages is— Imbecility; imbecility in the vast majority of men, at all times, and, even in heroes, in all but certain eminent moments; victims of gravity, custom, and fear. This gives force to the strong,—that the multitude have no habit of self-reliance or original action.

We must reckon success a constitutional trait. Courage,—the old physicians taught, (and their meaning holds, if their physiology is a little mythical,)—courage, or the degree of life, is as the degree of circulation of the blood in the arteries. Where the arteries hold their blood, is courage and adventure possible. Where they pour it unrestrained into the veins, the spirit is low and feeble. For performance of great mark, it needs extraordinary health. If Eric is in robust health, and has slept well, and is at the top of his condition, and thirty years old, at his departure from Greenland, he will steer west, and his ships will reach Newfoundland. But take out Eric, and put in a stronger and bolder man,—Biorn, or Thorfin,—and the ships will, with just as much ease, sail six hundred, one thousand, fifteen hundred miles further, and reach Labrador and New England. There is no chance in results. With adults, as with children, one class enter cordially into the game, and whirl with the whirling world; the others have cold hands, and remain bystanders; or are only dragged in by the humor and vivacity of those who can carry a dead weight. The first wealth is health. Sickness is poor-spirited, and cannot serve any one: it must husband its resources to live. But health or fulness answers its own ends, and has to spare, runs over, and inundates the neighborhoods and creeks of other men's necessities.

All power is of one kind, a sharing of the nature of the world. The mind that is parallel with the laws of nature will be in the current of events, and strong with their strength. One man is made of the same stuff of which events are made; is in sympathy with the course of things; can predict it. Whatever befalls, befalls him first; so that he is equal to whatever shall happen. A man who knows men, can talk well on politics, trade, law, war, religion. For, everywhere, men are led in the same manners.

The advantage of a strong pulse is not to be supplied by any labor, art, or concert. It is like the climate, which easily rears a crop, which no glass, or irrigation, or tillage, or manures, can elsewhere rival. It is like the opportunity of a city like New York, or Constantinople, which needs no diplomacy to force capital or genius or labor to it. They come of themselves, as the waters flow to it.

This affirmative force is in one, and is not in another, as one horse has the spring in him, and another in the whip. "On the neck of the young man," said Hafiz, "sparkles no gem so gracious as enterprise." Import into any stationary district, as into an old Dutch population in New York or Pennsylvania, or among the planters of Virginia, a colony of hardy Yankees, with seething brains, heads full of steam-hammer, pulley, crank, and toothed wheel,—and everything begins to shine with values. In every company, there is not only the active and passive sex, but, in both men and women, a deeper and more important *sex of mind*, namely, the inventive or creative class of both men and women, and the uninventive or accepting class. Each plus man represents his set, and, if he have the accidental advantage of personal ascendency,—which implies neither more nor less of talent, but merely the temperamental or taming eye of a soldier or a schoolmaster, (which one has, and one has not, as one has a black moustache and one a blond,) then quite easily and without envy or resistance, all his coadjutors and feeders will admit his right to absorb them.

There is always room for a man of force, and he makes room for many. Society is a troop of thinkers, and the best heads among them take the best places. A feeble man can see the farms that are fenced and tilled, the houses that are built. The strong man sees the possible houses and farms. His eye makes estates, as fast as the sun breeds clouds.

When a new boy comes into school, when a man travels, and encounters strangers every day, or, when into any old club a new comer is domesticated, that happens which befalls, when a strange ox is driven into a pen or pasture where cattle are kept; there is at once a trial of strength between the best pair of horns and the new comer, and it is settled thenceforth which is the leader. So now, there is a measuring of strength, very courteous, but decisive, and an acquiescence thenceforward when these two meet. Each reads his fate in the other's eyes. The weaker party finds, that none of his information or wit quite fits the occasion. He thought he knew this or that: he finds that he omitted to learn the end of it. Nothing that he knows will quite hit the mark, whilst all the rival's arrows are good, and well thrown. But if he knew all the facts in the encyclopaedia, it would not help him: for this is an affair of presence of mind, of attitude, of aplomb: the opponent has the sun and wind, and, in every cast, the choice of weapon and mark; and, when he himself is matched with some other antagonist, his own shafts fly well and hit. 'Tis a question of stomach and constitution. The second man is as good as the first,—perhaps better; but has not stoutness or stomach, as the first has, and so his wit seems over-fine or under-fine.

Health is good,—power, life, that resists disease, poison, and all enemies, and is conservative, as well as creative. Vivacity, leadership, must be had, and we are not allowed to be nice in choosing. And we have a certain instinct, that where is great amount of life, though gross and peccant, it has its own checks and purifications, and will be found at last in harmony with moral laws.

We prosper with such vigor, that, like thrifty trees, which grow in spite of ice, lice, mice, and borers, so we do not suffer from the profligate swarms. The huge animals nourish huge parasites, and the rancor of the disease attests the strength of the constitution.

All kinds of power usually emerge at the same time; good energy, and bad; power of mind, with physical health; the ecstasies of devotion, with the exasperations of debauchery. The same elements are always present, only sometimes these conspicuous, and sometimes those; what was yesterday foreground, being to-day background,—what was surface, playing now a not less effective part as basis. The longer the drought lasts, the more is the atmosphere surcharged with water. The faster the ball falls to the sun, the force to fly off is by so much augmented. And, in morals, wild liberty breeds iron conscience; natures with great impulses have great resources, and return from far. In politics, the sons of democrats will be whigs; whilst red republicanism, in the father, is a spasm of nature to engender an intolerable tyrant in the next age. On the other hand, conservatism, ever more timorous and narrow, disgusts the children, and drives them for a mouthful of fresh air into radicalism.

Those who have most of this coarse energy,—the 'bruisers,' who have run the gauntlet of caucus and tavern through the county or the state, have their own vices, but they have the good nature of strength and courage. Fierce and unscrupulous, they are usually frank and direct, and above falsehood. Our politics fall into bad hands, and churchmen and men of refinement, it seems agreed, are not fit persons to send to Congress. Politics is a deleterious profession, like some poisonous handicrafts. Men in power have no opinions, but may be had cheap for any opinion, for any purpose,—and if it be only a question between the most civil and the most forcible, I lean to the last.

In trade, also, this energy usually carries a trace of ferocity. Philanthropic and religious bodies do not commonly make their executive officers out of saints. The communities hitherto founded by Socialists,—the Jesuits, the Port-Royalists, the American communities at New Harmony, at Brook Farm, at Zoar, are only possible, by installing Judas as steward. The rest of the offices may be filled by good burgesses. The pious and charitable proprietor has a foreman not quite so pious and charitable. The most amiable of country gentlemen has a certain pleasure in the teeth of the bull-dog which guards his orchard. Of the Shaker society, it was formerly a sort of proverb in the country, that they always sent the devil to market. And in representations of the Deity, painting, poetry, and popular religion have ever drawn the wrath from Hell. It is an esoteric doctrine of society, that a little wickedness is good to make muscle; as if conscience were not good for hands and legs, as if poor decayed formalists of law and order cannot run like wild goats, wolves, and conies; that, as there is a use in medicine for poisons, so the world cannot move without rogues; that public spirit and the ready hand are as well found among the malignants. 'Tis not very rare, the coincidence of sharp private and political practice, with public spirit, and good neighborhood.

Whilst thus the energy for originating and executing work, deforms itself by excess, and so our axe chops off our own fingers,—this evil is not without remedy. All the elements whose aid man calls in, will sometimes become his masters, especially those of most subtle force. Shall he, then, renounce steam, fire, and electricity, or, shall he learn to deal with them? The rule for this whole class of agencies is,—all plus is good; only put it in the right place.

Men of this surcharge of arterial blood cannot live on nuts, herb-tea, and elegies; cannot read novels, and play whist; cannot satisfy all their wants at the Thursday Lecture, or the Boston Athenaeum. They pine for adventure, and must go to Pike's Peak; had rather die by the hatchet of a Pawnee, than sit all day and every day at a counting-room desk. They are made for war, for the sea, for mining, hunting, and clearing; for hair-breadth adventures, huge risks, and the joy of eventful living. Some men cannot endure an hour of calm at sea.

The excess of virility has the same importance in general history, as in private and industrial life. Strong race or strong individual rests at last on natural forces, which are best in the savage, who, like the beasts around him, is still in reception of the milk from the teats of Nature. Cut off the connection between any of our works, and this aboriginal source, and the work is shallow. The people lean on this, and the mob is not quite so bad an argument as we sometimes say, for it has this good side. "March without the people," said a French deputy from the tribune, "and you march into night: their instincts are a finger-pointing of Providence, always turned toward real benefit."

The best anecdotes of this force are to be had from savage life, in explorers, soldiers, and buccaneers. But who cares for fallings-out of assassins, and fights of bears, or grindings of icebergs? Physical force has no value, where there is nothing else. Snow in snow-banks, fire in volcanoes and solfataras is cheap. The luxury of ice is in tropical countries, and midsummer days. The luxury of fire is, to have a little on our hearth: and of electricity, not volleys of the charged cloud, but the manageable stream on the battery-wires.

In history, the great moment is, when the savage is just ceasing to be a savage, with all his hairy Pelasgic strength directed on his sense of beauty;—and you have Pericles and Phidias,—not yet passed over into the Corinthian civility. Everything good in nature and the world is in that moment of transition, when the swarthy juices still flow plentifully from nature, but their astringency or acridity is got out by ethics and humanity.

The triumphs of peace have been in some proximity to war. Whilst the hand was still familiar with the sword-hilt, whilst the habits of the camp were still visible in the port and complexion of the gentleman, his intellectual power culminated: the compression and tension of these stern conditions is a training for the finest and softest arts, and can rarely be compensated in tranquil times, except by some analogous vigor drawn from occupations as hardy as war.

We say that success is constitutional; depends on a *plus* condition of mind and body, on power of work, on courage; that it is of main efficacy in carrying on the world, and, though rarely found in the right state for an article of commerce, but oftener in the supersaturate or excess, which makes it dangerous and destructive, yet it cannot be spared, and must be had in that form, and absorbents provided to take off its edge.

The affirmative class monopolize the homage of mankind. They originate and execute all the great feats. What a force was coiled up in the skull of Napoleon! Of the sixty thousand men making his army at Eylau, it seems some thirty thousand were thieves and burglars. The men whom, in peaceful communities, we hold if we can, with iron at their legs, in prisons, under the muskets of sentinels, this man dealt with, hand to hand, dragged them to their duty, and won his victories by their bayonets.

This aboriginal might gives a surprising pleasure when it appears under conditions of supreme refinement, as in the proficients in high art. When Michel Angelo was forced to paint the Sistine Chapel in fresco, of which art he knew nothing, he went down into the Pope's gardens behind the Vatican, and with a shovel dug out ochres, red and yellow, mixed them with glue and water with his own hands, and having, after many trials, at last suited himself, climbed his ladders, and painted away, week after week, month after month, the sibyls and prophets. He surpassed his successors in rough vigor, as much as in purity of intellect and refinement. He was not crushed by his one picture left unfinished at last. Michel was wont to draw his figures first in skeleton, then to clothe them with flesh, and lastly to drape them. "Ah!" said a brave painter to me, thinking on these things, "if a man has failed, you will find he has dreamed instead of working. There is no way to success in our art, but to take off your coat, grind paint, and work like a digger on the railroad, all day and every day."

Success goes thus invariably with a certain *plus* or positive power: an ounce of power must balance an ounce of weight. And, though a man cannot return into his mother's womb, and be born with new amounts of vivacity, yet there are two economies, which are the best *succedanea* which the case admits. The first is, the stopping off decisively our miscellaneous activity, and concentrating our force on one or a few points; as the gardener, by severe pruning, forces the sap of the tree into one or two vigorous limbs, instead of suffering it to spindle into a sheaf of twigs.

"Enlarge not thy destiny," said the oracle: "endeavor not to do more than is given thee in charge." The one prudence in life is concentration; the one evil is dissipation: and it makes no difference whether our dissipations are coarse or fine; property and its cares, friends, and a social habit, or politics, or music, or feasting. Everything is good which takes away one plaything and delusion more, and drives us home to add one stroke of faithful work. Friends, books, pictures, lower duties, talents, flatteries, hopes,—all are distractions which cause oscillations in our giddy balloon, and make a good poise and a straight course impossible. You must elect your work; you shall take what your brain can, and drop all the rest. Only so, can that amount of vital force accumulate, which can make the step from knowing to doing. No matter how much faculty of idle seeing a man has, the step from knowing to doing is rarely taken. 'Tis a step out of a chalk circle of imbecility into fruitfulness. Many an artist lacking this, lacks all: he sees the masculine Angelo or Cellini with despair. He, too, is up to Nature and the First Cause in his thought. But the spasm to collect and swing his whole being into one act, he has not. The poet Campbell said, that "a man accustomed to work was equal to any achievement he resolved on, and, that, for himself, necessity not inspiration was the prompter of his muse."

Concentration is the secret of strength in politics, in war, in trade, in short, in all management of human affairs. One of the high anecdotes of the world is the reply of Newton to the inquiry, "how he had been able to achieve his discoveries?"—"By always intending my mind." Or if you will have a text from politics, take this from Plutarch: "There was, in the whole city, but one street in which Pericles was ever seen, the street which led to the market-place and the council house. He declined all invitations to banquets, and all gay assemblies and company. During the whole period of his administration, he never dined at the table of a friend." Or if we seek an example from trade,—"I hope," said a good man to Rothschild, "your children are not too fond of money and business: I am sure you would not wish that."—"I am sure I should wish that: I wish them to give mind, soul, heart, and body to business,—that is the way to be happy. It requires a great deal of boldness and a great deal of caution, to make a great fortune, and when you have got it, it requires ten times as much wit to keep it. If I were to listen to all the projects proposed to me, I should ruin myself very soon. Stick to one business, young man. Stick to your brewery, and you will be the great brewer of London. Be brewer, and banker, and merchant, and manufacturer, and you will soon be in the Gazette."

Many men are knowing, many are apprehensive and tenacious, but they do not rush to a decision. But in our flowing affairs a decision must be made,—the best, if you can; but any is better than none. There are twenty ways of going to a point, and one is the shortest; but set out at once on one. A man who has that presence of mind which can bring to him on the instant all he knows, is worth for action a dozen men who know as much, but can only bring it to light slowly. The good Speaker in the House is not the man who knows the theory of parliamentary tactics, but the man who decides off-hand. The good judge is not he who does hair-splitting justice to every allegation, but who, aiming at substantial justice, rules something intelligible for the guidance of suitors. The good lawyer is not the man who has an eye to every side and angle of contingency, and qualifies all his qualifications, but who throws himself on your part so heartily, that he can get you out of a scrape. Dr. Johnson said, in one of his flowing sentences, "Miserable beyond all names of wretchedness is that unhappy pair, who are doomed to reduce beforehand to the principles of abstract reason all the details of each domestic day. There are cases where little can be said, and much must be done."

The second substitute for temperament is drill, the power of use and routine. The hack is a better roadster than the Arab barb. In chemistry, the galvanic stream, slow, but continuous, is equal in power to the electric spark, and is, in our arts, a better agent. So in human action, against the spasm of energy, we offset the continuity of drill. We spread the same amount of force over much time, instead of condensing it into a moment. 'Tis the same ounce of gold here in a ball, and there in a leaf. At West Point, Col. Buford, the chief engineer, pounded with a hammer on the trunnions of a cannon, until he broke them off. He fired a piece of ordnance some hundred times in swift succession, until it burst. Now which stroke broke the trunnion? Every stroke. Which blast burst the piece? Every blast. The worst provincial company of actors would go through a play better than the best amateur company. The worst regular troops will beat the best volunteers. Practice is nine tenths. A course of mobs is good practice for orators. All the great speakers were bad speakers at first. Stumping it through England for seven years, made Cobden a consummate debater. Stumping it through New England for twice seven, trained Wendell Phillips. The way to learn German, is, to read the same dozen pages over and over a hundred times, till you know every word and particle in them, and can pronounce and repeat them by heart. No genius can recite a ballad at first reading, so well as mediocrity can at the fifteenth or twentieth reading. A humorous friend of mine thinks, that the reason why Nature is so perfect in her art, and gets up such inconceivably fine sunsets, is, that she has learned how, at last, by dint of doing the same thing so very often. Cannot one converse better on a topic on which he has experience, than on one which is new? Hence the use of drill, and the worthlessness of amateurs to cope with practitioners. Six hours every day at the piano, only to give facility of touch; six hours a day at painting, only to give command of the odious materials, oil, ochres, and brushes. The masters say, that they know a master in music, only by seeing the pose of the hands on the keys;—so difficult and vital an act is the command of the instrument. To have learned the use of the tools, by thousands of manipulations; to have learned the arts of reckoning, by endless adding and dividing, is the power of the mechanic and the clerk.

I remarked in England, in confirmation of a frequent experience at home, that, in literary circles, the men of trust and consideration, bookmakers, editors, university deans and professors, bishops, too, were by no means men of the largest literary talent, but usually of a low and ordinary intellectuality, with a sort of mercantile activity and working talent. Indifferent hacks and mediocrities tower, by pushing their forces to a lucrative point, or by working power, over multitudes of superior men.

I have not forgotten that there are sublime considerations which limit the value of talent and superficial success. We can easily overpraise the vulgar hero. There are sources on which we have not drawn. I know what I abstain from. But this force or spirit, being the means relied on by Nature for bringing the work of the day about,—as far as we attach importance to household life, and the prizes of the world, we must respect that. And I hold, that an economy may be applied to it; it is as much a subject of exact law and arithmetic as fluids and gases are; it may be husbanded, or wasted; every man is efficient only as he is a container or vessel of this force, and never was any signal act or achievement in history, but by this expenditure. This is not gold, but the gold-maker; not the fame, but the exploit.

If these forces and this husbandry are within reach of our will, and the laws of them can be read, we infer that all success, and all conceivable benefit for man, is also, first or last, within his reach, and has its own sublime economies by which it may be attained. The world is mathematical, and has no casualty, in all its vast and flowing curve. Success has no more eccentricity, than the gingham and muslin we weave in our mills. I know no more affecting lesson to our busy, plotting New England brains, than to go into one of the factories with which we have lined all the watercourses in the States. A man hardly knows how much he is a machine, until he begins to make telegraph, loom, press, and locomotive, in his own image. But in these, he is forced to leave out his follies and hindrances, so that when we go to the mill, the machine is more moral than we. Let a man dare go to a loom, and see if he be equal to it. Let machine confront machine, and see how they come out.

The world-mill is more complex than the calico-mill, and the architect stooped less. In the gingham-mill, a broken thread or a shred spoils the web through a piece of a hundred yards, and is traced back to the girl that wove it, and lessens her wages. The stockholder, on being shown this, rubs his hands with delight. Are you so cunning, Mr. Profitloss, and do you expect to swindle your master and employer, in the web you weave? A day is a more magnificent cloth than any muslin, the mechanism that makes it is infinitely cunninger, and you shall not conceal the sleezy, fraudulent, rotten hours you have slipped into the piece, nor fear that any honest thread, or straighter steel, or more inflexible shaft, will not testify in the web.

ABOUT THE AUTHORS

Born in 1803 in Boston, Massachusetts, RALPH WALDO EMERSON was one of America's preeminent men of letters. The inspiration for the school of philosophy called Transcendentalism, Emerson, in his essays, journals, lectures, and letters, traced out a view of life that located man as an extension and reflection of the Divine, owing his existence and allegiance to none but the highest insights of his own nature. An inspiration on figures ranging from his contemporary Henry David Thoreau to William James, Emerson formulated what can be called the American spiritual vision: non-dogmatic, nonsectarian, and based in the integrity and primacy of the individual spiritual search. In that sense, Emerson is also the founding figure of much of the modern spiritual culture in the West. After many years as a writer, publisher, lecturer, and seeker, he died in 1882 in Concord, Massachusetts, where his house still stands today.

MITCH HOROWITZ is the PEN Award-winning author of books including *Occult America* and *The Miracle Club*. A writer-in-residence at the New York Public Library and lecturer-in-residence at the University of Philosophical Research in Los Angeles, Mitch introduces and edits G&D Media's line of Condensed Classics and is the author of the Napoleon Hill Success Course series, including *The Miracle of a Definite Chief Aim* and *The Power of the Master Mind*. Visit him at Mitch-Horowitz.com.

THE
ART OF WAR

THE ART
OF WAR

by Sun Tzu

*History's Greatest Work on
Strategy—Now in a Special
Condensation*

Abridged and Introduced
by Mitch Horowitz

THE CONDENSED CLASSICS LIBRARY™

Contents

The Unlikeliest Classic

By Mitch Horowitz

Since its first creditable English translation in 1910, the ancient Chinese martial text *The Art of War* has enthralled Western readers. First gaining the attention of military officers, sinologists, martial artists, and strategy aficionados, *The Art of War* is today read by business executives, athletes, artists, and seekers from across the self-help spectrum. This is a surprising destiny for a work on ancient warfare estimated to be written around 500 BC by Zhou dynasty general Sun Tzu, an honorific title meaning "Master Sun." Very little is known about the author other than a historical consensus that such a figure actually existed as a commander in the dynastic emperor's army.

What, then, accounts for the enduring popularity of a text that might have been conscripted to obscurity in the West?

Like the best writing from the Taoist tradition, *The Art of War* is exquisitely simple, practical, and clear. Its insights into life and its inevitable conflicts are so organic and sound—Taoism is based on aligning with the natural order of things—that many people who have never been on a battlefield are immediately drawn into wanting to apply Sun Tzu's maxims to daily life.

Indeed, this gentle condensation is intended to highlight those aphorisms and lessons that have the broadest general applicability. I have no doubt that as you experience this volume you will immediately discover ideas that you want to note and use. This is because Sun Tzu's genius as a writer is to return us to natural principles—things that we may have once understood intuitively but lost in superfluous and speculative analysis, another of life's inevitabilities.

I have based this abridgment on the aforementioned and invaluable 1910 English translation by British sinologist Lionel Giles. Giles' translation has stood up with remarkable relevance over the past century. Rather than laden his words with the flourish of late-Victorian prose, Giles honored the starkness and sparseness of the original work. I have occasionally altered an obscure or antiquated term, but, overall, the economy and elegance of Giles' translation is an art form in itself, and deserves to be honored as such.

Why then a condensation at all? In some instances, Sun Tzu, a working military commander, necessarily touched upon battlefield intricacies—such as the fine points of terrain or attacking the enemy with fire—that prove less immediately applicable to modern life than his observations on the movements and motives of men. In a few spots I also add a clarifying note to bring out Sun Tzu's broader points.

I ask the reader to take special note of Sun Tzu's frequent references to adhering to the natural landscape. It is a classically Taoist approach to blend with the curvature and qualities of one's surroundings—to find your place in the organic order of things. Within the Vedic tradition this is sometimes called dharma. Transcendentalist philosopher Ralph Waldo Emerson also notes the need to cycle yourself with the patterns of nature. As the great Hermetic dictum put it: "As above, so below."

Another key to Sun Tzu's popularity is the manner in which he unlocks the universality of true principles. What applies in warfare, if authentic, must apply to other areas of life. Human nature is consistent. So are the ebb and flow of events, on both macro and intimate levels. Be on the watch for this principle throughout the text.

Another central aspect of Sun Tzu's thought—again in harmony with Taoism—is that the greatest warrior prevails without ever fighting. If a fighter has observed conditions, deciphered the enemy, and diligently prepared and marshaled his forces, the ideal is to overwhelm his foe without shooting a single arrow. "Supreme excellence," Sun Tzu writes, "consists in breaking the enemy's resistance without fighting."

If an attack does prove necessary, it should be launched with irresistible force, like a seismic shifting of the earth. After your enemy's defeat, quickly return to normalcy. "In war then," the master writes, "let your object be victory, not lengthy campaigns." Sun Tzu warns against protracted operations. "There is no instance of a country having benefited from prolonged warfare," he writes.

Rather than seek glory, Sun Tzu counsels that the excellent commander practices subtlety, inscrutability, watchfulness, and flexibility. The good fighter, he writes, should be like water: dwelling unnoticed at his enemy's lowest depths and then striking with overwhelming power at his weakest points, the way a torrent of water rushes downhill. This constitutes ideal preparation and formation for attack: practice patience, carefully study the enemy, know his limits and strengths and your own, never be lured or tricked into battle—and then strike with ferocity. And never fight unless victory is assured.

If I had to put *The Art of War* into a nutshell, I would use this one of the master's maxims: "Let your plans be dark and impenetrable as night, and when you move, fall like a thunderbolt."

In a sense, *The Art of War* is about unlearning the complexities of life and returning to the simple and true. This voice from millennia ago can teach us how to strip away obfuscation. May its wisdom bring you your highest effectiveness.

CHAPTER I

Laying Plans

Sun Tzu said: The art of war is of vital importance to the State.

It is a matter of life and death, a road either to safety or to ruin. Hence, it is a subject of inquiry that can on no account be neglected.

The art of war, then, is governed by five constant factors, to be taken into account in one's deliberations when seeking to determine the conditions obtaining in the field.

These are:

(1) The Moral Law;

(2) Heaven;

(3) Earth;

(4) The Commander;

(5) Method and Discipline.

The Moral Law causes the people to be in complete accord with their ruler, so that they will follow him regardless of their lives, undismayed by any danger.

Heaven signifies night and day, cold and heat, times and seasons.

Earth comprises distances, great and small; danger and security; open ground and narrow passes; the chances of life and death.

The Commander stands for the virtues of wisdom, sincerity, benevolence, courage, and strictness.

By method and discipline are to be understood the marshaling of the army in its proper subdivisions, the graduations of rank among the officers, the maintenance of roads by which supplies may reach the army, and the control of military expenditure.

These five heads should be familiar to every general: he who knows them will be victorious; he who knows them not will fail.

Therefore, in your deliberations, when seeking to determine the military conditions, let them be made the basis of a comparison, in this way:

(1) Which of the two sovereigns is imbued with the Moral Law?

(2) Which of the two generals has most ability?

(3) With whom lie the advantages derived from Heaven and Earth?

(4) On which side is discipline most rigorously enforced?

(5) Which army is stronger?

(6) On which side are officers and men more highly trained?

(7) In which army is there the greater constancy both in reward and punishment?

By means of these seven considerations I can forecast victory or defeat.

The general that hearkens to my counsel and acts upon it, will conquer: let such a one be retained in command! The general that hearkens not to my counsel nor acts upon it, will suffer defeat—let such a one be dismissed!

While heeding the profit of my counsel, avail yourself also of any helpful circumstances over and beyond the ordinary rules.

According as circumstances are favorable, one should modify one's plans.

All warfare is based on deception.

Hence, when able to attack, we must seem unable; when using our forces, we must seem inactive; when we are near, we must make the enemy believe we are far away; when far away, we must make him believe we are near.

Hold out baits to entice the enemy. Feign disorder, and crush him.

If he is secure at all points, be prepared for him. If he is in superior strength, evade him.

If your opponent is bad-tempered, seek to irritate him. Pretend to be weak, that he may grow arrogant.

If he is at ease, give him no rest. If his forces are united, separate them.

Attack him where he is unprepared, appear where you are not expected.

These military devices, leading to victory, must not be divulged beforehand.

Now the general who wins a battle makes many calculations in his temple ere the battle is fought. The general who loses a battle makes but few calculations beforehand. Thus do many calculations lead to victory, and few calculations to defeat: how much more no calculation at all! It is by attention to this point that I can foresee who is likely to win or lose.

CHAPTER II

Waging War

When you engage in actual fighting, if victory is long in coming, then men's weapons will grow dull and their ardor will be dampened. If you lay siege to a town, you will exhaust your strength.

Again, if the campaign is protracted, the resources of the State will not be equal to the strain.

Now, when your weapons are dulled, your ardor dampened, your strength exhausted and your treasure spent, other chieftains will spring up to take advantage of your extremity. Then no man, however wise, will be able to avert the consequences that must ensue.

Thus, though we have heard of stupid haste in war, cleverness has never been seen associated with long delays.

There is no instance of a country having benefited from prolonged warfare.

It is only one who is thoroughly acquainted with the evils of war that can thoroughly understand the profitable way of carrying it on.

The skillful soldier does not levy a second tax, neither are his supply-wagons loaded more than twice.

Bring war material with you from home, but forage on the enemy. Thus the army will have food enough for its needs.

Poverty of the State treasury causes an army to be maintained by contributions from a distance. Contributing to maintain an army at a distance causes the people to be impoverished.

On the other hand, the proximity of an army causes prices to go up; and high prices cause the people's substance to be drained away.

When their substance is drained away, the peasantry will be afflicted by heavy exactions.

With this loss of substance and exhaustion of strength, the homes of the people will be stripped bare, and three-tenths of their income will be dissipated; while government expenses for broken chariots, worn-out horses, breast-plates and helmets, bows and arrows, spears and shields, protective mantles, draught-oxen and heavy wagons, will amount to four-tenths of its total revenue.

Hence a wise general makes a point of foraging on the enemy. One cartload of the enemy's provisions is equivalent to twenty of one's own, and likewise a single parcel from his stores is equivalent to twenty from one's own stores.

Now in order to kill the enemy, our men must be roused to anger; that there may be advantage from defeating the enemy, they must have their rewards.

Therefore in chariot fighting, when ten or more chariots have been taken, those should be rewarded who took the first. Our own flags should be substituted for those of the enemy, and the chariots mingled and used in conjunction with ours. The captured soldiers should be kindly treated and kept.

This is called, using the conquered foe to augment one's own strength.

In war, then, let your great object be victory, not lengthy campaigns.

Thus it may be known that the leader of armies is the arbiter of the people's fate, the man on whom it depends whether the nation shall be in peace or in peril.

Chapter III

Attack by Stratagem

Sun Tzu said: In the practical art of war, the best thing of all is to take the enemy's country whole and intact; to shatter and destroy it is not so good. So, too, it is better to recapture an army entire than to destroy it, to capture a regiment, a detachment or a company entire than to destroy them.

Hence to fight and conquer in all your battles is not supreme excellence; supreme excellence consists in breaking the enemy's resistance without fighting.

Thus the highest form of generalship is to block the enemy's plans; the next best is to prevent the junction of the enemy's forces; the next in order is to attack the enemy's army in the field; and the worst policy of all is to besiege walled cities.

The rule is, not to besiege walled cities if it can possibly be avoided. The preparation of mantlets, movable shelters, and various implements of war, will take up three whole months; and the piling up of mounds over against the walls will take three months more.

The general, unable to control his irritation, will launch his men to the assault like swarming ants, with the result that one-third of his men are slain, while the town still remains untaken. Such are the disastrous effects of a siege.

Therefore the skillful leader subdues the enemy's troops without any fighting; he captures their cities without laying siege to them; he overthrows their kingdom without lengthy operations in the field.

With his forces intact he will dispute the mastery of the Empire, and thus, without losing a man, his triumph will be complete. This is the method of attacking by stratagem.

It is the rule in war, if our forces are ten to the enemy's one, to surround him; if five to one, to attack him; if twice as numerous, to divide our army into two.

If equally matched, we can offer battle; if slightly inferior in numbers, we can avoid the enemy; if quite unequal in every way, we can flee from him.

Hence, though an obstinate fight may be made by a small force, in the end it must be captured by the larger force.

Now the general is the bulwark of the State; if the bulwark is complete at all points, the State will be strong; if the bulwark is defective, the State will be weak.

There are three ways in which a ruler can bring misfortune upon his army:

(1) By commanding the army to advance or to retreat, being ignorant of the fact that it cannot obey. This is called hobbling the army.

(2) By attempting to govern an army in the same way as he administers a kingdom, being ignorant of the conditions which obtain in an army. This causes restlessness in the soldiers' minds.

(3) By employing the officers of his army without discrimination, through ignorance of the military principle of adaptation to circumstances. This shakes the confidence of the soldiers.

But when the army is restless and distrustful, trouble is sure to come from the other feudal princes. This is simply bringing anarchy into the army, and flinging victory away.

Thus we may know that there are five essentials for victory:

(1) He will win who knows when to fight and when not to fight.

(2) He will win who knows how to handle both superior and inferior forces.

(3) He will win whose army is animated by the same spirit throughout all its ranks.

(4) He will win who, prepared himself, waits to take the enemy unprepared.

(5) He will win who has military capacity and is not interfered with by the sovereign.

Hence the saying: If you know the enemy and know yourself, you need not fear the result of a hundred battles. If you know yourself but not the enemy, for every victory gained you will also suffer a defeat. If you know neither the enemy nor yourself, you will succumb in every battle.

Chapter IV

Tactical Dispositions

S un Tzu said: The good fighters of old first put themselves beyond the possibility of defeat, and then waited for an opportunity of defeating the enemy.

To secure ourselves against defeat lies in our own hands, but the opportunity of defeating the enemy is provided by the enemy himself.

Thus the good fighter is able to secure himself against defeat, but cannot make certain of defeating the enemy.

Hence the saying: One may know how to conquer without being able to do it.*

Security against defeat implies defensive tactics; ability to defeat the enemy means taking the offensive.

---

* This is natural law: where two parties are involved the outcome depends on both.—MH

Standing on the defensive indicates insufficient strength; attacking, a superabundance of strength.

The general who is skilled in defense hides in the most secret recesses of the earth; he who is skilled in attack flashes forth from the topmost heights of heaven. Thus on the one hand we have ability to protect ourselves; on the other, a victory that is complete.

To see victory only when it is within the ken of the common herd is not the acme of excellence.

Neither is it the acme of excellence if you fight and conquer and the whole Empire says, "Well done!"

To lift an autumn hair is no sign of great strength; to see the sun and moon is no sign of sharp sight; to hear the noise of thunder is no sign of a quick ear.

What the ancients called a clever fighter is one who not only wins, but excels in winning with ease.

Hence his victories bring him neither reputation for wisdom nor credit for courage.

He wins his battles by making no mistakes. Making no mistakes is what establishes the certainty of victory, for it means conquering an enemy that is already defeated.

Hence the skillful fighter puts himself into a position which makes defeat impossible, and does not miss the moment for defeating the enemy.

Thus it is that in war the victorious strategist only seeks battle after the victory has been won, whereas he who is destined to defeat first fights and afterwards looks for victory.

The consummate leader cultivates the moral law, and strictly adheres to method and discipline; thus it is in his power to control success.*

In respect of military method, we have, firstly, Measurement; secondly, Estimation of quantity; thirdly, Calculation; fourthly, Balancing of chances; fifthly, Victory.

Measurement owes its existence to Earth; Estimation of quantity to Measurement; Calculation to Estimation of quantity; Balancing of chances to Calculation; and Victory to Balancing of chances.

A victorious army opposed to a routed one, is as a pound's weight placed in the scale against a single grain.

The onrush of a conquering force is like the bursting of pent-up waters into a chasm a thousand fathoms deep.

---

* It is useful here to note that Sun Tzu adheres not to inspiration, which can come and go, but to "method and discipline," where are permanent.—MH

Chapter V

Energy

S un Tzu said: The control of a large force is the same principle as the control of a few men: it is merely a question of dividing up their numbers.

Fighting with a large army under your command is in no way different from fighting with a small one: it is merely a question of instituting signs and signals.

To ensure that your whole army may withstand the brunt of the enemy's attack and remain unshaken—this is effected by maneuvers direct and indirect.

That the impact of your army may be like a grindstone dashed against an egg—this is effected by the science of weak points and strong.

In all fighting, the direct method may be used for joining battle, but indirect methods will be needed in order to secure victory.

Indirect tactics, efficiently applied, are inexhaustible as Heaven and Earth, unending as the flow of rivers and streams; like the sun and moon, they end but to begin anew; like the four seasons, they pass away to return once more.*

There are not more than five musical notes, yet the combinations of these five give rise to more melodies than can ever be heard.

There are not more than five primary colors (blue, yellow, red, white, and black), yet in combination they produce more hues than can ever been seen.

There are not more than five cardinal tastes (sour, acrid, salt, sweet, bitter), yet combinations of them yield more flavors than can ever be tasted.

In battle, there are not more than two methods of attack—the direct and the indirect; yet these two in combination give rise to an endless series of maneuvers.

The direct and the indirect lead on to each other in turn. It is like moving in a circle—you never come to an end. Who can exhaust the possibilities of their combination?

The onset of troops is like the rush of a torrent, which will even roll stones along in its course.

---

* This precept should be read and contemplated carefully with the one immediately preceding it.—MH

The quality of decision is like the well-timed swoop of a falcon, which enables it to strike and destroy its victim.

Therefore the good fighter will be terrible in his onset, and prompt in his decision.

Energy may be likened to the bending of a crossbow; decision, to the releasing of a trigger.

Amid the turmoil and tumult of battle, there may be seeming disorder and yet no real disorder at all; amid confusion and chaos, your array may be without head or tail, yet it will be proof against defeat.

Simulated disorder postulates perfect discipline, simulated fear postulates courage; simulated weakness postulates strength.

Hiding order beneath the cloak of disorder is simply a question of subdivision; concealing courage under a show of timidity presupposes a fund of latent energy; masking strength with weakness is to be effected by tactical dispositions.

Thus one who is skillful at keeping the enemy on the move maintains deceitful appearances, according to which the enemy will act. He sacrifices something, that the enemy may snatch at it.

By holding out baits, he keeps him on the march; then with a body of picked men he lies in wait for him.

The clever combatant looks to the effect of combined energy, and does not require too much from individuals. Hence his ability to pick out the right men and utilize combined energy.*

When he utilizes combined energy, his fighting men become as it were like unto rolling logs or stones. For it is the nature of a log or stone to remain motionless on level ground, and to move when on a slope; if four-cornered, to come to a standstill, but if round-shaped, to go rolling down.

Thus the energy developed by good fighting men is as the momentum of a round stone rolled down a mountain thousands of feet in height.

---

* Sun Tzu is saying that you must not over-rely on any one person or factor.—MH

Chapter VI

Weak Points and Strong

S un Tzu said: Whoever is first in the field and awaits the coming of the enemy, will be fresh for the fight; whoever is second in the field and has to hasten to battle will arrive exhausted.*

Therefore the clever combatant imposes his will on the enemy, but does not allow the enemy's will to be imposed on him.

By holding out advantages to him, he can cause the enemy to approach of his own accord; or, by inflicting damage, he can make it impossible for the enemy to draw near.

If the enemy is taking his ease, he can harass him; if well supplied with food, he can starve him out; if quietly encamped, he can force him to move.

---

* This is one of Sun Tzu's most practical lessons: always arrive first.—MH

Appear at points that the enemy must hasten to defend; march swiftly to places where you are not expected.

An army may march great distances without distress, if it marches through country where the enemy is not.

You can be sure of succeeding in your attacks if you only attack places that are undefended. You can ensure the safety of your defense if you only hold positions that cannot be attacked.

Hence that general is skillful in attack whose opponent does not know what to defend; and he is skillful in defense whose opponent does not know what to attack.

O divine art of subtlety and secrecy! Through you we learn to be invisible, through you inaudible; and hence we can hold the enemy's fate in our hands.

You may advance and be absolutely irresistible, if you make for the enemy's weak points; you may retire and be safe from pursuit if your movements are more rapid than those of the enemy.

If we wish to fight, the enemy can be forced to an engagement even though he be sheltered behind a high rampart and a deep ditch. All we need do is attack some other place that he will be obliged to relieve.

If we do not wish to fight, we can prevent the enemy from engaging us even though the lines of our encampment be merely traced out on the ground. All we need do is to throw something odd and unaccountable in his way.

By discovering the enemy's dispositions and remaining invisible ourselves, we can keep our forces concentrated, while the enemy's must be divided.

We can form a single united body, while the enemy must split up into fractions. Hence there will be a whole pitted against separate parts of a whole, which means that we shall be many to the enemy's few.

And if we are able thus to attack an inferior force with a superior one, our opponents will be in dire straits.

The spot where we intend to fight must not be made known; for then the enemy will have to prepare against a possible attack at several different points; and his forces being thus distributed in many directions, the numbers we shall have to face at any given point will be proportionately few.

For should the enemy strengthen his approach, he will weaken his rear; should he strengthen his rear, he will weaken his approach; should he strengthen his left, he will weaken his right; should he strengthen his right, he will weaken his left. If he sends reinforcements everywhere, he will everywhere be weak.

Numerical weakness comes from having to prepare against possible attacks; numerical strength, from compelling our adversary to make these preparations against us.

Knowing the place and the time of the coming battle, we may concentrate from the greatest distances in order to fight.

Though the enemy be stronger in numbers, we may prevent him from fighting. Scheme so as to discover his plans and the likelihood of their success.

Rouse him, and learn the principle of his activity or inactivity. Force him to reveal himself, so as to find out his vulnerable spots.

Carefully compare the opposing army with your own, so that you may know where strength is superabundant and where it is deficient.

In making tactical dispositions, the highest pitch you can attain is to conceal them; conceal your dispositions, and you will be safe from the prying of the subtlest spies, from the machinations of the wisest brains.

How victory may be produced for them out of the enemy's own tactics—that is what the multitude cannot comprehend.

All men can see the tactics whereby I conquer, but what none can see is the strategy out of which victory is evolved.

Do not repeat the tactics that have gained you one victory, but let your methods be regulated by the infinite variety of circumstances.

Military tactics are like unto water; for water in its natural course runs away from high places and hastens downwards.

So in war, the way is to avoid what is strong and to strike at what is weak.

Water shapes its course according to the nature of the ground over which it flows; the soldier works out his victory in relation to the foe that he is facing.*

Therefore, just as water retains no constant shape, so in warfare there are no constant conditions.

He who can modify his tactics in relation to his opponent and thereby succeed in winning, may be called a heaven-born captain.

The five elements (water, fire, wood, metal, earth) are not always equally predominant; the four seasons make way for each other in turn. There are short days and long; the moon has its periods of waning and waxing.

---

* Sun Tzu is counseling flexibility, morphing, and response to changed circumstances. Do not be rigid.—MH

Chapter VII

Maneuvering

Sun Tzu said: In war, the general receives his commands from the sovereign.

Having collected an army and concentrated his forces, he must blend and harmonize the different elements thereof before pitching his camp.

After that, comes tactical maneuvering, than which there is nothing more difficult. The difficulty of tactical maneuvering consists in turning the devious into the direct, and misfortune into gain.

Thus, to take a long and circuitous route, after enticing the enemy out of the way, and though starting after him, to contrive to reach the goal before him, shows knowledge of the artifice of DEVIATION.

Maneuvering with an army is advantageous; with an undisciplined multitude, most dangerous.

If you set a fully equipped army to march in order to snatch an advantage, the chances are that you will be too late. On the other hand, to detach a flying column for the purpose involves the sacrifice of its baggage and stores.

Thus, if you order your men to roll up their buff-coats, and make forced marches without halting day or night, covering double the usual distance at a stretch in order to wrest an advantage, the leaders of all your three divisions will fall into the hands of the enemy.

The stronger men will be in front, the jaded ones will fall behind, and on this plan only one-tenth of your army will reach its destination.

If you march long distances to outmaneuver the enemy, you will lose the leader of your first division, and only half your force will reach the goal. Even you modify the long distance, two-thirds of your army will arrive.

Hence it follows that an army without its baggage-train is lost; without provisions it is lost; without bases of supply it is lost.

We cannot enter into alliances until we are acquainted with the designs of our neighbors.

We are not fit to lead an army on the march unless we are familiar with the face of the country—its mountains and forests, its pitfalls and precipices, its marshes and swamps.

We shall be unable to turn natural advantage to account unless we make use of local guides.

In war, practice concealment, and you will succeed.

Whether to concentrate or to divide your troops, must be decided by circumstances.

Let your rapidity be that of the wind, your compactness that of the forest.

In raiding and plundering be like fire, as immovability is like a mountain.

Let your plans be dark and impenetrable as night, and when you move, fall like a thunderbolt.

When you plunder a countryside, let the spoils be divided amongst your men; when you capture new territory, cut it up into allotments for the benefit of the soldiery.

Ponder and deliberate before you make a move.

He will conquer who has learnt the artifice of deviation. Such is the art of maneuvering.

The Book of Army Management says: On the field of battle, the spoken word does not carry far enough: hence the institution of gongs and drums. Nor can ordinary objects be seen clearly enough: hence the institution of banners and flags.

Gongs and drums, banners and flags, are means whereby the ears and eyes of the army may be focused on one particular point.

The army thus forming a single united body, it is impossible either for the brave to advance alone, or for the cowardly to retreat alone. This is the art of handling large masses of men.

In night-fighting, then, make much use of signal-fires and drums, and in fighting by day, of flags and banners, as a means of influencing the ears and eyes of your army.

A whole army may be robbed of its spirit; a commander-in-chief may be robbed of his presence of mind.

Now a soldier's spirit is keenest in the morning; by noonday it has begun to flag; and in the evening, his mind is bent only on returning to camp.

A clever general, therefore, avoids an army when its spirit is keen, but attacks it when it is sluggish and inclined to return. This is the art of studying moods.

Disciplined and calm, to await the appearance of disorder and hubbub amongst the enemy—this is the art of retaining self-possession.

To be near the goal while the enemy is still far from it, to wait at ease while the enemy is toiling and struggling, to be well-fed while the enemy is famished—this is the art of husbanding one's strength.

To refrain from intercepting an enemy whose banners are in perfect order, to refrain from attacking an army drawn up in calm and confident array—this is the art of studying circumstances.

It is a military axiom not to advance uphill against the enemy, nor to oppose him when he comes downhill.

Do not pursue an enemy who simulates flight; do not attack soldiers whose temper is keen.

Do not swallow bait offered by the enemy. Do not interfere with an army that is returning home.

When you surround an army, leave an outlet free. Do not press a desperate foe too hard.*

Such is the art of warfare.

---

* By pressing a desperate foe, and leaving him no way out, you ensure he will fight to the death.—MH

CHAPTER VIII

Variation in Tactics

S un Tzu said: In war, the general receives his commands from the sovereign, collects his army, and
concentrates his forces

When in difficult country, do not encamp. In country where high roads intersect, join hands with your allies. Do not linger in dangerously isolated positions. In
hemmed-in situations, you must resort to stratagem. In
desperate position, you must fight.

There are roads that must not be followed, armies
that must be not attacked, towns that must be besieged,
positions that must not be contested, commands of the
sovereign that must not be obeyed.

The general who thoroughly understands the advantages that accompany variation of tactics knows
how to handle his troops.

The general who does not understand these may be
well acquainted with the configuration of the country,

yet he will not be able to turn his knowledge to practical account.

So, the student of war who is unversed in the art of war of varying his plans, even though he is acquainted with the Five Advantages, will fail to make the best use of his men.*

Hence in the wise leader's plans, considerations of advantage and of disadvantage will be blended together.

If our expectation of advantage is tempered in this way, we may succeed in accomplishing the essential part of our schemes.

If, on the other hand, in the midst of difficulties we are always ready to seize an advantage, we may extricate ourselves from misfortune.

Reduce the hostile chiefs by inflicting damage on them; and make trouble for them, and keep them constantly engaged; hold out specious allurements, and make them rush to any given point.

The art of war teaches us to rely not on the likelihood of the enemy's not coming, but on our own readiness to receive him; not on the chance of his not attacking, but rather on the fact that we have made our position unassailable.

---

* For the "Five Advantages," see Sun Tzu's note on the "five essentials for victory" in chapter III.—MH

There are five dangerous faults which may affect a general:

    (1) Recklessness, which leads to destruction;

    (2) cowardice, which leads to capture;

    (3) a hasty temper, which can be provoked by insults;

    (4) a delicacy of honor which is sensitive to shame;

    (5) over-solicitude for his men, which exposes him to worry and trouble.

These are the five besetting sins of a general, ruinous to the conduct of war.

When an army is overthrown and its leader slain, the cause will surely be found among these five dangerous faults. Let them be a subject of meditation.

CHAPTER IX

The Army on the March

S un Tzu said: We come now to the question of encamping the army, and observing signs of the enemy. Pass quickly over mountains, and keep in the neighborhood of valleys.

Camp in high places, facing the sun. Do not climb heights in order to fight.

After crossing a river, you should get far away from it.

When an invading force crosses a river in its onward march, do not advance to meet it in midstream. It will be best to let half the army get across, and then deliver your attack.

If you are anxious to fight, you should not go to meet the invader near a river that he has to cross.*

---

* In these passages, Sun Tzu is staying that you must exhaust your enemy by enticing him to cross a river.—MH

Moor your craft higher up than the enemy, and facing the sun. Do not move upstream to meet the enemy.

In crossing saltmarshes, your sole concern should be to get over them quickly, without any delay.

If forced to fight in a saltmarsh, you should have water and grass near you, and get your back to a clump of trees.

In dry, level country, take up an easily accessible position with rising ground to your right and on your rear, so that the danger may be in front, and safety lie behind.

All armies prefer high ground to low and sunny places to dark.

If you are careful of your men, and camp on hard ground, the army will be free from disease of every kind, and this will spell victory.

When you come to a hill or a bank, occupy the sunny side, with the slope on your right rear. Thus you will at once act for the benefit of your soldiers and utilize the natural advantages of the ground.

When, in consequence of heavy rains up-country, a river you wish to ford is swollen and flecked with foam, you must wait until it subsides.

Country in which there are precipitous cliffs with torrents running between, deep natural hollows, confined places, tangled thickets, quagmires and crevasses, should be left with all possible speed and not approached.

While we keep away from such places, we should get the enemy to approach them; while we face them, we should let the enemy have them on his rear.

If in the neighborhood of your camp there should be any hilly country, ponds surrounded by aquatic grass, hollow basins filled with reeds, or woods with thick undergrowth, they must be carefully routed out and searched; for these are places where men in ambush or insidious spies are likely to be lurking.

When the enemy is close at hand and remains quiet, he is relying on the natural strength of his position.

When he keeps aloof and tries to provoke a battle, he is anxious for the other side to advance.

If his place of encampment is easy of access, he is tendering a bait.

Movement amongst the trees of a forest shows that the enemy is advancing. The appearance of a number of screens in the midst of thick grass means that the enemy wants to make us suspicious.

The rising of birds in their flight is the sign of an ambush. Startled beasts indicate that a sudden attack is coming.

Humble words and increased preparations are signs that the enemy is about to advance. Violent language and driving forward as if to the attack are signs that he will retreat.

When the light chariots come out first and take up a position on the wings, it is a sign that the enemy is forming for battle.

Peace proposals unaccompanied by a sworn covenant indicate a plot.

When there is much running about and the soldiers fall into rank, it means that the critical moment has come.

When some are seen advancing and some retreating, it is a lure.

When the soldiers stand leaning on their spears, they are faint from want of food.

If those who are sent to draw water begin by drinking themselves, the army is suffering from thirst.

If the enemy sees an advantage to be gained and makes no effort to secure it, the soldiers are exhausted.

If birds gather on any spot, it is unoccupied. Clamor by night betokens nervousness.

If there is disturbance in the camp, the general's authority is weak. If the banners and flags are shifted about, sedition is afoot. If the officers are angry, it means that the men are weary.

When an army feeds its horses with grain and kills its cattle for food, and when the men do not hang their cooking-pots over the camp-fires, showing that they will not return to their tents, you may know that they are determined to fight to the death.*

The sight of men whispering together in small knots or speaking in subdued tones points to disaffection amongst the rank and file.

Too frequent rewards signify that the enemy is at the end of his resources; too many punishments betray a condition of dire distress.

To begin by bluster, but afterwards to take fright at the enemy's numbers, shows a supreme lack of intelligence.

When envoys are sent with compliments in their mouths, it is a sign that the enemy wishes for a truce.

If the enemy's troops march up angrily and remain facing ours for a long time without either joining battle or taking themselves off again, the situation is one that demands great vigilance and circumspection.

If our troops are no more in number than the enemy that is amply sufficient; it only means that no direct attack can be made. What we can do is simply to concentrate all our available strength, keep a close watch on the enemy, and obtain reinforcements.

---

* Men eat grain; horses eat grass. Hence, the slaying of cattle means a preparation for the end.—MH

He who exercises no forethought but makes light of his opponents is sure to be captured by them.

If soldiers are punished before they have grown attached to you, they will not prove submissive; and, unless submissive, then will be practically useless. If, when the soldiers have become attached to you, punishments are not enforced, they will still be useless.

Therefore soldiers must be treated in the first instance with humanity, but kept under control by means of iron discipline. This is a certain road to victory.

If in training soldiers commands are habitually enforced, the army will be well disciplined; if not, its discipline will be bad.

If a general shows confidence in his men but always insists on his orders being obeyed, the gain will be mutual.

CHAPTER X

Dangers and Opportunities

Now an army is exposed to six varying calamities, not arising from natural causes, but from faults for which the general is responsible. These are: (1) flight; (2) insubordination; (3) collapse; (4) ruin; (5) disorganization; (6) rout.

Other conditions being equal, if one force is hurled against another ten times its size, the result will be the flight of the former.

When the common soldiers are too strong and their officers too weak, the result is insubordination. When the officers are too strong and the common soldiers too weak, the result is collapse.

When the higher officers are angry and insubordinate, and on meeting the enemy give battle on their own account from a feeling of resentment, before the commander-in-chief can tell whether or not he is in a position to fight, the result is ruin.

When the general is weak and without authority; when his orders are not clear and distinct; when there are no fixed duties assigned to officers and men, and the ranks are formed in a slovenly haphazard manner, the result is utter disorganization.

When a general, unable to estimate the enemy's strength, allows an inferior force to engage a larger one, or hurls a weak detachment against a powerful one, and neglects to place picked soldiers in the front rank, the result must be rout.

These are six ways of courting defeat, which must be carefully noted by the general who has attained a responsible post.

The natural formation of the country is the soldier's best ally; but a power of estimating the adversary, of controlling the forces of victory, and of shrewdly calculating difficulties, dangers, and distances, constitutes the test of a great general.

He who knows these things, and in fighting puts his knowledge into practice, will win his battles. He who knows them not, nor practices them, will surely be defeated.

If fighting is sure to result in victory, then you must fight, even though the ruler forbid it; if fighting will not result in victory, then you must not fight, even at the ruler's bidding.

The general who advances without coveting fame and retreats without fearing disgrace, whose only thought is to protect his country and do good service for his sovereign, is the jewel of the kingdom.

Regard your soldiers as your children, and they will follow you into the deepest valleys; look upon them as your own beloved sons, and they will stand by you even unto death.

If, however, you are indulgent, but unable to make your authority felt; kind-hearted, but unable to enforce your commands; and incapable, moreover, of quelling disorder: then your soldiers must be likened to spoilt children; they are useless for any practical purpose.

If we know that our own men are in a condition to attack, but are unaware that the enemy is not open to attack, we have gone only halfway towards victory.

If we know that the enemy is open to attack, but are unaware that our own men are not in a condition to attack, we have gone only halfway towards victory.

If we know that the enemy is open to attack, and also know that our men are in a condition to attack, but are unaware that the nature of the ground makes fighting impracticable, we have still gone only halfway towards victory.

Hence the experienced soldier, once in motion, is never bewildered; once he has broken camp, he is never at a loss.

Hence the saying: If you know the enemy and know yourself, your victory will not stand in doubt; if you know Heaven and know Earth, you may make your victory complete.

If asked how to cope with a great army of the enemy in orderly array and on the point of marching to the attack, I should say: "Begin by seizing something which your opponent holds dear; then he will be amenable to your will."

Rapidity is the essence of war: take advantage of the enemy's unreadiness, make your way by unexpected routes, and attack unguarded spots.

The following are the principles to be observed by an invading force: The further you penetrate into a country, the greater will be the solidarity of your troops, and thus the defenders will not prevail against you.

Make forays in fertile country in order to supply your army with food.

Carefully study the wellbeing of your men, and do not overtax them. Concentrate your energy and hoard your strength. Keep your army continually on the move, and devise unfathomable plans.

Throw your soldiers into positions whence there is no escape, and they will prefer death to flight. If they will face death, there is nothing they may not achieve. Officers and men alike will put forth their uttermost strength.

Soldiers when in desperate straits lose the sense of fear. If there is no place of refuge, they will stand firm. If they are in hostile country, they will show a stubborn front. If there is no help for it, they will fight hard.

Thus, without waiting to be marshaled, the soldiers will be constantly on the alert; without waiting to be asked, they will do your will; without restrictions, they will be faithful; without giving orders, they can be trusted.

Prohibit the taking of omens, and do away with superstitious doubts. Then, until death itself comes, no calamity need be feared.

If our soldiers are not overburdened with money, it is not because they have a distaste for riches; if their lives are not unduly long, it is not because they are disinclined to longevity.

On the day they are ordered out to battle, your soldiers may weep. But let them once be brought to bay, and they will display great courage.

The principle on which to manage an army is to set up one standard of courage which all must reach.

How to make the best of both strong and weak—that is a question involving the proper use of ground.

Thus the skillful general conducts his army just as though he were leading a single man, in all places, by the hand.

It is the business of a general to be quiet and thus ensure secrecy; upright and just, and thus maintain order.

He must be able to mystify his officers and men by false reports and appearances, and thus keep them in total ignorance.

By altering his arrangements and changing his plans, he keeps the enemy without definite knowledge. By shifting his camp and taking circuitous routes, he prevents the enemy from anticipating his purpose.

At the critical moment, the leader of an army acts like one who has climbed up a height and then kicks away the ladder behind him. He carries his men deep into hostile territory before he shows his hand.

He burns his boats and breaks his cooking-pots; like a shepherd driving a flock of sheep, he drives his men this way and that, and nothing knows whither he is going.*

To muster his army and bring it into danger—this may be termed the business of the general.

It is the soldier's disposition to offer an obstinate resistance when surrounded, to fight hard when he cannot help himself, and to obey promptly when he has fallen into danger.

We cannot enter into alliance with neighboring princes until we are acquainted with their designs. We are not fit to lead an army on the march unless we are familiar with the face of the country—its mountains and forests, its pitfalls and precipices, its marshes and swamps. We shall be unable to turn natural advantages to account unless we make use of local guides.

To be ignorant of any one of the following four or five principles does not befit a warlike prince.

When a warlike prince attacks a powerful state, his generalship shows itself in preventing the concentration of the enemy's forces. He overawes his opponents, and their allies are prevented from joining against him.

---

* The reference to burning boats and breaking cooking pots is akin to the Western expression to "burn the fleet"—in other words, to eliminate any way out and thus to guarantee victory or demise. This also makes a show of determination to troops and foes.—MH

Hence he does not strive to ally himself with all and sundry, nor does he foster the power of other states. He carries out his own secret designs, keeping his antagonists in awe. Thus he is able to capture their cities and overthrow their kingdoms.

Bestow rewards without regard to rule, issue orders without regard to previous arrangements; and you will be able to handle a whole army as though you had to do with but a single man.

Confront your soldiers with the deed itself; never let them know your design. When the outlook is bright, bring it before their eyes; but tell them nothing when the situation is gloomy.*

Place your army in deadly peril, and it will survive; plunge it into desperate straits, and it will come off in safety.

For it is precisely when a force has fallen into harm's way that is capable of striking a blow for victory.

Success in warfare is gained by carefully accommodating ourselves to the enemy's purpose.

By persistently hanging on the enemy's flank, we shall succeed in the long run in killing the commander-in-chief.

---

* In the first part of this principle, Sun Tzu is saying to focus troops on the goal not on the means to the goal.—MH

This is called ability to accomplish a thing by sheer cunning.

If the enemy leaves a door open, you must rush in.

Forestall your opponent by seizing what he holds dear, and subtly contrive to time his arrival on the ground.

Walk in the path defined by rule, and accommodate yourself to the enemy until you can fight a decisive battle.

At first, then, exhibit the coyness of a maiden, until the enemy gives you an opening; afterwards emulate the rapidity of a running hare, and it will be too late for the enemy to oppose you.

Unhappy is the fate of one who tries to win his battles and succeed in his attacks without cultivating the spirit of enterprise; for the result is waste of time and general stagnation.

Hence the saying: The enlightened ruler lays his plans well ahead; the good general cultivates his resources.

Move not unless you see an advantage; use not your troops unless there is something to be gained; fight not unless the position is critical.

No ruler should put troops into the field merely to gratify his own spleen; no general should fight a battle simply out of irritation.

If it is to your advantage, make a forward move; if not, stay where you are.

Anger may in time change to gladness; vexation may be succeeded by content.

But a kingdom that has once been destroyed can never come again into being; nor can the dead ever be brought back to life.

Hence the enlightened ruler is heedful, and the good general full of caution. This is the way to keep a country at peace and an army intact.

Chapter XI

The Use of Spies

Hostile armies may face each other for years, striving for the victory that is decided in a single day. This being so, to remain in ignorance of the enemy's condition simply because one grudges the outlay of a hundred ounces of silver in honors and payments is the height of inhumanity.

One who acts thus is no leader of men, no present help to his sovereign, no master of victory.

Thus, what enables the wise sovereign and the good general to strike and conquer, and achieve things beyond the reach of ordinary men, is foreknowledge.

Now this foreknowledge cannot be elicited from spirits; it cannot be obtained inductively from experience, nor by any deductive calculation.

Knowledge of the enemy's dispositions can only be obtained from other men.

Spies cannot be usefully employed without a certain intuitive sagacity.

They cannot be properly managed without benevolence and straightforwardness.

Without subtle ingenuity of mind, one cannot make certain of the truth of their reports.

Be subtle! be subtle! and use your spies for every kind of business.

Whether the object be to crush an army, to storm a city, or to assassinate an individual, it is always necessary to begin by finding out the names of the attendants, the aides-de-camp, and doorkeepers and sentries of the general in command. Our spies must be commissioned to ascertain these.

The enemy's spies who have come to spy on us must be sought out, tempted with bribes, led away, and comfortably housed. Thus they will become converted spies and available for our service.

About the Authors

Little is known about Sun Tzu, who is estimated to have been born in 544 BC in the latter-era of China's Zhou dynasty, and died in 496 BC. Historians generally agree that Sun Tzu—an honorific title meaning "Master Sun"—was a commander in the dynastic army. His ancient treatise on strategy is one of the most widely read works of antiquity.

Lionel Giles, whose groundbreaking 1910 translation of Sun Tzu is used in this abridgment, was a British sinologist and curator who also translated the works of Confucius and Lao Tzu. Born in 1875, he died in 1958.

Mitch Horowitz is the PEN Award-winning author of books including *Occult America* and *The Miracle Club*. A writer-in-residence at the New York Public Library and lecturer-in-residence at the University of Philosophical Research in Los Angeles, Mitch introduces and edits G&D Media's line of Condensed Classics and is the author of the Napoleon Hill Success Course series, including *The Miracle of a Definite Chief Aim* and *The Power of the Master Mind*. Visit him at MitchHorowitz.com.